Crazy Simple YouTube.

Coach Aaron Cuha

Table Of Contents

CHAPTER 1
The $387,000 YouTube Video

OPENING HOOK

Let's call him Marcus.

In 2019, Marcus was a real estate agent in Austin, Texas. Same grind as every other agent in his office. Cold calls before lunch. Open houses on weekends. Networking events where he'd rather gnaw his own arm off than hand out another business card. And underneath all of it, this low-level panic that the leads were about to dry up.

One Saturday afternoon, he skipped the open house. Grabbed his iPhone. Drove to a neighborhood he'd been working in for five years. No ring light. No lapel mic. No real plan. Just Marcus, his phone propped on the dashboard, and twenty minutes of real talk about why that neighborhood was perfect for young families.

He covered the school districts. The hidden park only locals knew about. The new coffee shop that had basically become the unofficial town hall. Price trends he'd watched shift over half a decade. He uploaded it, typed a quick description, and forgot about it.

Six years later, that single video has produced over $387,000 in closed commissions. It still generates leads while Marcus sleeps. And the kicker? It took forty-five minutes to create.

Not forty-five hours. Not forty-five days of planning, overthinking, and production meetings. Forty-five minutes from turning the key in the ignition to hitting publish. Crazy simple. And that simplicity is the entire point.

People relocating to Austin from California found that video. Families in New York researching neighborhoods at 11 PM while their kids slept found that video. Investors scouting rental properties found it too. Every single one of them found Marcus before they found his competitors. Because Marcus showed up on YouTube, and nobody else did.

THE FRAMEWORK

Who This Book Is For (And Why I Wrote It)

Before we go any further, let me tell you who's holding this book.

You're a real estate agent who's tired of cold calling and begging for referrals. Or you're a mortgage lender watching your pipeline dry up every time rates shift. Maybe you're a coach, consultant, financial advisor, contractor, or small business owner in a hundred other industries. The common thread? You know you need a better way to attract clients, and you've got a gut feeling YouTube might be it. But you don't know where to start. Or you started, and nothing happened.

This book is for you.

It's not for people who want to become YouTubers. It's not for people chasing fame, subscribers, or a silver play button on the wall. It's for people who run real businesses and want YouTube to become their most reliable, highest-quality lead generation engine. Period.

If that's you, you're in the right place. And you don't need to be technical, creative, or camera-ready to make this work. The system I'm about to give you was built for busy professionals who have two to three hours a week, a smartphone, and something valuable to say. That's the bar.

Why Me

I should probably tell you why I'm the one writing this.

I'm Aaron Cuha. I run two YouTube channels. @VanLife has over 120,000 subscribers. @GotCoach has over 50,000. Combined, that's 170,000+ subscribers built on the exact strategies in this book. I'm also a Tom Ferry coach and speaker, a licensed broker in 12 states, and I've logged over 15,000 hours of one-on-one coaching with business owners on YouTube growth.

But the credential that matters most? I use YouTube to run actual businesses. Not to teach YouTube. Not to sell courses about YouTube. To generate leads, close clients, and build revenue for real companies. Everything in this book comes from that lens. When I tell you something works, it's because I tested it on my own channels with my own money before I ever put it in front of a client.

My core philosophy is right there in the title: *Crazy Simple*. I believe YouTube growth has been overcomplicated by people who profit from making it seem harder than it is. The gurus. The course sellers. The "YouTube strategists" who have never generated a single client from a video. They turn a straightforward process into a maze of jargon and $997 programs. I'm here to strip all that away and give you the playbook that actually works.

Why YouTube Is a Different Animal

I need you to understand something that will change how you think about content forever.

YouTube is not TikTok. YouTube is not Instagram. YouTube is not Facebook.

On Instagram, you post a photo. Your followers see it. Engagement spikes for maybe 48 hours. Then it dies. You're back to zero. Every. Single. Post. It's a hamster wheel that never stops spinning, and you never get anywhere.

TikTok? You're fighting for attention against teenagers doing dance challenges. Your content might blow up. Or it might get 47 views. The algorithm over there is basically a slot machine, and no serious business owner should build a strategy around pulling a lever and hoping for the best.

YouTube works nothing like either of those platforms.

YouTube is the second-largest search engine on the planet. Bigger than Bing, Yahoo, and every other search engine combined. Second only to Google, which (not a coincidence) owns YouTube. When someone types "best neighborhoods in Austin for families" into that search bar, they aren't scrolling mindlessly. They're actively looking for an answer. They have a problem. They have intent. And if your video solves that problem, they will find you.

Not just today. Not just this week. For years.

Does that make sense? This is the single biggest difference between YouTube and everything else. Your content keeps working long after you publish it.

The YouTube Compound Effect

Let me walk you through what actually happens when you post a video on YouTube versus anywhere else.

Month one: Your video picks up a few views from search. YouTube's algorithm is testing it. Seeing if people actually watch past the first thirty seconds. Deciding whether to show it to more people.

Month three: If your retention numbers are solid (we'll get deep into this later), YouTube starts suggesting your video to a wider audience. Views climb. Slowly, but they climb.

Month six: Now your video ranks for search terms you didn't even target. It's showing up in the suggested videos sidebar next to your competitors' content. You're pulling their audience without spending a dollar on ads.

Year one: That single video has generated dozens of leads, multiple clients, and thousands of dollars in revenue. And it's not slowing down.

Year three: Hundreds of leads. Dozens of clients. The revenue equivalent of a full-time employee's salary. From one video.

Year six: Marcus is at $387,000 in commission from that Saturday afternoon iPhone recording. Still going.

That's the compound effect. Every video you create is a brick in a building that gets more valuable over time. While your competitors are stuck on the content treadmill, posting and posting and posting, starting from zero every single day, you're building something that appreciates. Like real estate, actually. Funny how that works.

And here's what really bends people's brains when they see it for the first time: the growth isn't linear. It's exponential. Your first ten videos might collectively generate 30 leads over a year. But videos 11 through 20 generate 80, because now YouTube trusts your channel. It knows your content keeps people watching. So it shows your newer videos to larger audiences faster. Videos 21 through 30? You're looking at 200+ leads. Same effort per video. Wildly different output.

I've watched this pattern play out on my own channels and across dozens of client channels. The people who quit at video eight because "nothing is happening" are standing right at the edge of the curve. They just can't see it yet.

The Authority Flywheel

There's a second thing happening at the same time that most business owners completely miss.

When a potential client watches your videos before they ever pick up the phone, something shifts. They already trust you. They've heard your voice. Seen your face. Watched you break down concepts with confidence. They might have consumed 10, 20, maybe 50 minutes of your content across multiple videos. By the time they reach out, you're not some stranger. You're the expert they've already chosen.

I call this the Authority Flywheel, and it runs on a simple loop:

Content leads to trust.

Trust leads to leads.

Leads become clients.

Clients give you more stories and expertise.

That expertise becomes more content.

The flywheel spins faster.

And the leads that come through this flywheel? They're not cold leads. They're not "I saw your ad" leads. They're warm, pre-sold, ready-to-go leads. The kind who say things like, "I've been watching your videos for months. I already know I want to work with you. I just needed to hear your voice on the phone to confirm it."

One of my coaching clients told me, "I used to chase clients. Now they chase me." That's the flywheel at work.

Think about what that does to your entire business model. You stop spending money on ads that generate cold leads who don't know you. You stop wasting Saturday mornings at open houses hoping someone walks in. You stop making 50 cold calls to get one lukewarm appointment. Instead, your phone rings, and the person on the other end already likes you, already trusts your expertise, and already decided to work with you before they ever dialed your number.

That's not a marketing improvement. That's a completely different business.

The 2026 Opportunity

So why now? Why is this book landing in your hands at this exact moment?

Because the window is still wide open. And most people in your industry are still standing on the wrong side of it.

YouTube has 2.5 billion monthly active users. The average session duration is over 40 minutes, which means people aren't just scrolling. They're sitting down and watching. AI tools have made professional-quality content accessible to everyone, even if you've never edited a video in your life. We'll cover all of that in this book.

But here's the number that should get your attention: in most industries, your direct competitors still aren't on YouTube. Real estate, coaching, consulting, financial services, legal, home services. They're either completely absent or doing it so poorly it barely counts. Short videos with no SEO. No strategy. No consistency.

I'm not saying this to create fake urgency. I'm saying it because I've watched it happen in real time. Markets where one agent starts a YouTube channel and, within 18 months, becomes the name everyone in town knows. Not because they spent the most on ads. Not because they had the best brokerage behind them. Because they showed up consistently in search results while everyone else argued about whether YouTube was "worth it."

The business owners who figure this out right now will own their markets for the next decade. That's not hype. That's math. And this book is going to show you exactly how to do it.

AI INTEGRATION

Your YouTube Business Case Builder

Before you create a single video, I want you to understand the potential ROI for your specific business. Not in theory. In real numbers.

Copy this prompt into ChatGPT or Claude and fill in the brackets with your information:

PROMPT: YouTube Business Case Builder

I'm a [YOUR PROFESSION] in [YOUR CITY/MARKET].

My average transaction/client value is $[AMOUNT].

My current conversion rate from lead to client is approximately [X]%.

Help me calculate:

1. If I create one video per week and each video generates an average of 2 leads per month after 6 months, what's my potential annual revenue from YouTube?
2. What is my 'YouTube Hourly Rate' if each video takes 2 hours to create?
3. Compare this ROI to my current marketing methods (cold calling, paid ads, networking events).
4. What's the 3-year compound value if my videos continue generating leads indefinitely?

Be specific with numbers. Show your math.

This exercise gives you a concrete number you can return to whenever you're tempted to skip a week of content. When you know each video is worth $5,000 or $10,000 or $50,000 over its lifetime, carving out two hours a week stops feeling like a sacrifice and starts feeling like the smartest investment you'll make all month.

CASE STUDY

The VanLife Laboratory: Zero to 120K Subscribers

In 2024, I launched a channel called @VanLife with one purpose: to test everything I teach.

I'd been coaching business owners on YouTube for years at that point. But I wanted a lab. A controlled environment where I could test theories, measure results, and either validate or disprove the strategies I was putting in front of my clients.

I picked VanLife because the content format mirrors business content almost perfectly. Van tours are property tours. Destination guides are neighborhood spotlights. Travel tips are educational content. If I could crack the code on a VanLife channel, every single lesson would transfer directly to my coaching clients' businesses.

So we started testing. And the results surprised even me.

Video length was the big one. Short videos (three to four minutes) grew the channel by 300 to 400 new subscribers per month. Fine. Not bad. Bump that to five minutes? Growth jumped to 500 to 2,000 new subscribers per month. But when we went deep, averaging around 18 minutes per video, we hit 5,000+ new subscribers per month.

Read that again. By going longer and going deeper, we 10x'd the growth rate. This flies in the face of the "short attention span" myth that keeps business owners creating weak little two-minute videos nobody watches.

We tested SEO strategies, thumbnail designs, title formulas, posting schedules, paid promotions, and hook structures. Every test generated data. Every result sharpened the system. Some of our assumptions turned out to be completely wrong, and that was the whole point. Better to find out on my channel than to give a client bad advice.

The thumbnail testing alone changed how I coach people. We found that faces outperformed text-only thumbnails by 3x in click-through rate. Bright backgrounds crushed dark ones. And the "curiosity gap" in titles (making the viewer feel compelled to click to get the answer) consistently outperformed straightforward descriptive titles. All of this is in the chapters ahead.

Today, @VanLife sits at over 120,000 subscribers. But subscriber count isn't the point. The point is that it validated every strategy you're about to read in this book. Nothing here is academic. Everything is battle-tested.

CRAZY SIMPLE ACTION

Calculate Your YouTube Hourly Rate

Before you flip to Chapter 2, I need you to do this. Five minutes. That's all it takes. And it will completely change how you think about content creation.

Grab a pen. Or open your notes app. And answer these four questions:

- What is your average client or transaction value? $__________
- If one YouTube video generates just ONE client per year, what is that video worth? $__________
- If that video keeps working for five years (and that's conservative), what is the lifetime value? $__________
- If creating that video takes three hours, what is your "YouTube Hourly Rate"? $__________ per hour

For most business owners, this number is a gut punch, in the best way. When a real estate agent realizes that a three-hour video investment can generate $50,000+ in lifetime commission, the "I don't have time" excuse evaporates on the spot.

And look, I know what you might be thinking. "But Aaron, my first videos are going to be terrible. Nobody's going to watch them." You're probably right. Your first videos will be rough. That's fine. The math still works because YouTube gives your content time to find its audience. A video that gets 12 views in month one can get 1,200 views by month six if the content answers a real question. We'll cover exactly how to make that happen.

YouTube isn't a time expense. It's a time investment. And the returns compound over time. That's what makes it crazy simple. Not easy. Simple. A clear process, repeated consistently, that builds something bigger than any ad campaign or networking event ever could.

Write your YouTube Hourly Rate on a sticky note and put it somewhere you'll see it every single day. That number is your anchor when creating content feels hard, when you don't want to hit record, when imposter syndrome creeps in. Look at the number. Then press record anyway.

The Road Ahead

Here's what the rest of this book is going to do for you.

Part One lays the foundation. We'll destroy the myths holding you back, decode how the 2026 algorithm actually works, build your business model around YouTube, get your equipment sorted (for far less money than you think), and set up a channel that converts visitors into leads.

Part Two is where we build your content engine. Finding topics people are actually searching for. Crafting titles and thumbnails that get clicks. Writing hooks that stop the scroll. Structuring videos for maximum retention. Scripting your delivery. Editing for engagement. This is the core of the system.

Part Three turns your channel into a business asset. Publishing strategy, content calendars, analytics that matter, YouTube Shorts, lead generation systems, and converting those leads into paying clients.

Part Four scales everything. Building a team. Expanding your revenue streams. Growing your community. Repurposing content across platforms. Measuring real ROI. And your 90-day launch plan to put it all into action.

Every chapter follows the same format: a real story, the tactical framework, AI tools you can use immediately, a case study with real results, and an action step you can complete in one sitting. No theory for the sake of theory. No filler. Just the system, chapter by chapter, until you have a YouTube channel that works as hard as you do.

Forty-five minutes. That's how long it took Marcus to create a $387,000 asset. Your version starts right now.

In Chapter 2, we're going to tear apart the myths that are sabotaging most YouTube channels. The guru advice that sounds smart but actually kills your growth. You're going to be surprised by how much of what you've heard is flat-out wrong.

CHAPTER 2
Why Most YouTube Advice Is Wrong

OPENING HOOK

Daniel Kotula was doing everything the YouTube gurus told him to do.

Posting three times a week. Obsessing over subscriber count. Chasing trending topics that had nothing to do with his actual business. He'd watched every "How to Grow on YouTube" video he could find, taken notes like a college freshman, and followed the playbook to the letter.

Six months in, he had 247 subscribers and zero clients from YouTube. Not one.

Daniel runs a consulting business out of Prague. Smart guy. Great at what he does. But he'd fallen into the same trap that catches about 90% of business owners who try YouTube: he was taking advice from people who make money teaching YouTube, not from people who use YouTube to run an actual business.

There's a massive difference between those two things. And until you understand that difference, you'll keep spinning your wheels, making content that looks right, feels productive, and generates absolutely nothing.

I know because I've logged over 15,000 hours of one-on-one coaching sessions with business owners, and the same bad advice shows up in almost every first conversation. The myths are everywhere. They sound logical. They get millions of views on YouTube advice channels. And they are quietly destroying your chances of building a channel that actually makes you money.

Let's burn them down.

THE FRAMEWORK

Myth #1: You Need to Post Every Day

This is the one that burns people out faster than anything else. Some guru with a ring light and a leased Lamborghini told you that consistency means daily uploads. That the algorithm rewards volume. That if you're not posting every single day, you're falling behind.

Wrong.

YouTube's algorithm in 2026 does not care how often you post. It cares how long people watch. That's the metric that moves the needle. A channel posting one exceptional video per week will outperform a channel posting daily mediocre content every single time. I've seen it happen on my own channels and across dozens of client channels.

On @VanLife, we tested this directly. We ran a stretch of five uploads per week for a month, then dropped to two uploads per week the following month. The two-per-week period generated more total watch time, more subscribers, and more engagement. Why? Because we had time to actually make each video good. The scripts were tighter. The hooks were sharper. The thumbnails received more attention. Quality won.

The math is simple. If you post seven videos a week and each one gets watched for an average of three minutes, that's 21 minutes of total watch time per viewer. If you post two videos a week and each one gets watched for 12 minutes, that's 24 minutes. The algorithm sees 24 minutes and says, "This channel keeps people on the platform longer. Show it to more people."

Does that make sense? It's not about volume. It's about cumulative watch time per viewer. One great video beats five forgettable ones.

For business owners starting out, I recommend one video per week. That's it. One. Put all your energy into making that single video the best it can be. Better hook, better content, better thumbnail. You can scale to two per week once you have a system. But starting with daily uploads is the fastest path to quitting by month three.

Myth #2: Subscribers Are the Most Important Metric

Daniel was obsessed with his subscriber count. He checked it every morning like a stock ticker. Every new subscriber felt like progress. Every day without growth felt like failure.

Subscribers are a vanity metric. I'll say it louder for the people in the back.

Subscribers are a vanity metric.

In 2026, YouTube shows your videos to people based on their interests and behavior, not on whether they hit the subscribe button. A video can go viral and reach millions of people who have never heard of your channel. Meanwhile, plenty of your subscribers will never see your next upload because the algorithm decided it wasn't relevant to them that day.

The metrics that actually matter for business owners are watch time, click-through rate, and average view duration. These three numbers tell you whether your content is reaching people, whether they're clicking on it, and whether they're sticking around once they do. We'll go deep into analytics in Chapter 15, but for now, I need you to stop checking your subscriber count and start paying attention to how long people watch your videos.

A channel with 500 subscribers and a 50% average view duration will generate more leads than a channel with 50,000 subscribers and a 15% average view duration. Every time. The small channel is creating content that holds attention. The big channel has a number that looks impressive, and a business that's starving.

Myth #3: You Need Expensive Equipment to Start

We'll cover equipment in detail in Chapter 5, so I won't belabor this. But the myth needs to die right here.

Your iPhone shoots in 4K. The built-in microphone is good enough for your first 20 videos. Natural light from a window often looks better on camera than a cheap ring light. And free editing software like CapCut or DaVinci Resolve can do 95% of what a $300 subscription to Adobe Premiere can do.

I've seen agents spend $3,000 on camera gear before recording a single video. Then they quit two months later because the content didn't perform. The gear wasn't the problem. The strategy was. If you're spending more time researching microphones than researching what your audience actually searches for on YouTube, your priorities are upside down.

Start with your phone. Upgrade when the channel demands it. Not before.

Myth #4: Short Videos Are Better Because of Short Attention Spans

This one drives me crazy because it sounds so logical on the surface. "People have short attention spans these days, so make your videos short!" It gets repeated so often that most business owners accept it as fact without ever questioning it.

The data says the opposite.

On @VanLife, our longest videos consistently outperform our shortest ones in every metric that matters. Videos averaging 18 minutes generated 5,000+ new subscribers per month. Videos at three to four minutes? 300 to 400. That's not a small difference. That's a 10x gap.

And it makes sense when you think about what YouTube is trying to do. YouTube is an attention platform. It makes money when people stay on the platform longer. So which video does YouTube want to promote: the one that keeps someone watching for two minutes, or the one that keeps them watching for fifteen?

Now, there's a catch. Longer doesn't automatically mean better. A twenty-minute video that loses 80% of viewers in the first two minutes is worse than a five-minute video that holds 70% of its audience to the end. Length only wins when the content earns the watch time. But the myth that you should keep everything under five minutes because "people don't have patience" is flat wrong.

Your audience has plenty of patience for content that solves their problems. They'll watch a 30-minute video about the best neighborhoods in their target city if the information is genuinely useful. What they won't do is sit through two minutes of fluff. It's not about length. It's about value per minute.

Myth #5: You Need to Go Viral to Succeed

The viral dream is the most dangerous myth on this list. Not because going viral is bad, but because chasing virality will wreck your strategy.

Viral videos attract random audiences. They bring in viewers who have zero interest in your business, your market, or your services. A real estate agent in Denver who makes a funny video that goes viral might get 500,000 views from teenagers in Brazil. Cool for the ego. Worthless for the business.

The channels that generate real revenue don't chase viral moments. They build searchable libraries. They create content around the specific questions their ideal clients are already typing into YouTube's search bar. "Best neighborhoods in Denver for families." "How much house can I afford on a $100K salary?" "Moving to Denver from California, what to expect."

These videos might get 500 views in their first week. But they get 500 of the right views. And those views compound month after month, year after year. A video about Denver neighborhoods will still attract relocating families five years from now. A viral dance video will be forgotten by Thursday.

Small audiences that convert beat massive audiences that don't. Every single time.

Scott Himelstein proved this with his channel. He had not even 2,000 subscribers when he started closing deals directly from YouTube. His videos ranked for hyper-local search terms in his market. The people who found them were actively looking to buy or sell. Subscriber count? Irrelevant. Lead quality? Through the roof.

Myth #6: The Algorithm Is Working Against You

I hear this constantly. "The algorithm buried my video." "YouTube doesn't show my content to anyone." "The algorithm hates small channels."

No. The algorithm is the most sophisticated content recommendation engine ever built, and it has one job: keep people watching. If your video keeps people watching, the algorithm will show it to more people. If your video makes people click away, the algorithm will stop showing it. That's it. There's no conspiracy against small channels. There's no secret club you need to join.

The algorithm is actually your biggest ally as a business owner because it rewards exactly the kind of content you should be making: educational, specific, search-optimized content that answers real questions. The kind of content that holds attention because it delivers genuine value. If you're making that content and it's not performing, the issue isn't the algorithm. It's your titles, your thumbnails, your hooks, or your content structure. All fixable. All covered in the chapters ahead.

Stop blaming the algorithm. Start studying what it rewards. Those are two very different mindsets, and only one of them will grow your channel.

AI INTEGRATION

The Myth Buster Audit

Here's a prompt you can use right now to audit whether your current YouTube strategy is built on bad advice. If you haven't started yet, run this with your planned strategy and catch the mistakes before you make them.

PROMPT: YouTube Strategy Myth Audit

I'm a [YOUR PROFESSION] in [YOUR MARKET] planning my YouTube strategy. Here's what I'm currently doing or planning to do:

- Posting frequency: [X times per week]

- Average video length: [X minutes]

- Primary goal metric: [subscribers/views/other]

- Content approach: [describe your topics]

- Equipment budget: [$ amount]

Based on current YouTube algorithm behavior in 2026, audit this strategy for common myths and mistakes.

Specifically flag if I'm:

1. Prioritizing volume over quality

2. Chasing vanity metrics instead of watch time and retention

3. Over-investing in equipment before validating my content strategy

4. Making videos too short to build authority

5. Targeting broad/viral topics instead of searchable niche content

6. Blaming the algorithm instead of optimizing titles, thumbnails, and hooks

Give me a revised strategy that avoids these traps.

Be specific with numbers and timelines.

This takes three minutes and might save you six months of wasted effort. Run it before you record your next video.

CASE STUDY

Daniel Kotula: From 247 Subscribers to a Real Business

Let's come back to Daniel.

When Daniel first reached out to me, he was ready to quit YouTube. Six months of work. 247 subscribers. Zero clients. He'd been posting three times a week, covering trending business topics, using clickbait titles, and focusing entirely on subscriber growth.

The first thing I told him was, "Stop making videos for strangers. Start making videos for the specific people who will pay you money."

We rebuilt his strategy from scratch. Instead of chasing trending topics, we identified the 20 questions his ideal consulting clients were already searching for on YouTube. Instead of posting three times a week, we dropped to once a week and used the extra time to make each video genuinely useful. Instead of tracking subscribers, we started tracking average view duration and lead form submissions.

We changed his titles from clever and catchy to clear and searchable. "5 Business Hacks You Need to Know" became "How to Structure a Consulting Business in Europe: Step by Step." Less sexy. Way more effective.

Within 90 days, his average view duration jumped from 1:45 to 6:30. His videos started ranking on the first page for search terms his competitors weren't even targeting. And the leads started showing up. Not tire-kickers who found him through a trending topic. Real prospects who had searched for exactly the problem Daniel solves, watched him explain the solution for eight minutes, and then clicked the link in his description to book a call.

Daniel's channel still isn't huge by YouTube guru standards. But it generates consistent consulting leads from clients across Europe. That was always the point. Not fame. Revenue. He stopped following guru advice, started following a business-first strategy, and everything changed.

CRAZY SIMPLE ACTION

The Myth Detox

Grab your phone and open YouTube Studio (or your notes app if you haven't started your channel yet). We're doing a five-minute detox.

- Write down the three YouTube "rules" you've been following or planning to follow. Where did you learn each one? Was it from someone who uses YouTube to run a business, or someone who makes money teaching YouTube? Be honest.

- If you have existing videos, pull up your analytics. What is your average view duration on your last five videos? If it's under 40% of the total video length, your content strategy needs work, not your posting frequency.

- Pick the single most important question your ideal client would type into YouTube's search bar. Not a trending topic. Not something clever. The actual words a real person with a real problem would search for. Write that question down. That's your next video topic.

- Delete one myth from your strategy. If you've been posting daily and burning out, give yourself permission to go to once a week. If you've been making two-minute videos because someone told you attention spans are short, plan a ten-minute deep dive instead. If you've been obsessing over subscriber count, stop checking it for 30 days. Pick one myth and cut it loose.

This isn't busywork. This is a reset. Every myth you carry into your YouTube strategy is dead weight slowing you down. Drop it now so the chapters ahead can actually stick.

In Chapter 3, we're cracking open the 2026 YouTube algorithm. Not the theory. Not the speculation. The actual mechanics of how YouTube decides which videos to show, to whom, and why. Once you understand how the machine works, you can build content the machine wants to promote.

CHAPTER 3
The 2026 YouTube Algorithm Decoded

OPENING HOOK

In early 2026, YouTube quietly changed everything.

There was no press release. No big announcement at a creator conference. Just a series of algorithm updates rolled out over a few weeks, and suddenly creators who had been coasting started watching their views collapse. Channels that had grown steadily for years flatlined overnight. Panic spread through YouTube communities as people scrambled to figure out what had happened.

Meanwhile, a smaller group of creators noticed something completely different. Their videos were exploding. Content that had been performing "okay" was suddenly pulling 2x, 3x, even 5x the usual impressions. Subscriber growth accelerated. Revenue climbed.

Same platform. Same month. Wildly different outcomes.

The difference wasn't luck. It was understanding what YouTube actually optimizes for. And this latest round of updates made the algorithm's priorities impossible to miss.

YouTube stopped rewarding content that tricks people into clicking and started rewarding content that makes people glad they clicked.

That might sound like a small distinction. It's not. The clickbait era is dying. The "hack the algorithm" mentality is becoming obsolete. And creators who genuinely serve their audience, who create content people actually want to watch, are being rewarded like never before.

For business channels, this is the best news imaginable. Because serving your audience is exactly what authority content does. The algorithm finally caught up to what we've been teaching all along.

But to take advantage of this shift, you need to understand exactly how the algorithm thinks. Not the myths. Not the oversimplifications your competitor read in a blog post in 2021. The actual mechanics of how YouTube decides which videos to show to which viewers.

THE FRAMEWORK

How YouTube Actually Decides What to Show

YouTube's algorithm has one job: keep people on the platform as long as possible while ensuring they enjoy the experience enough to come back tomorrow.

That's it. Everything else flows from that single objective.

To accomplish this, YouTube tracks an enormous amount of data on every video and every viewer. But for creators, there are five metrics that matter most. These are the numbers that directly influence whether your videos get pushed to more viewers or buried where no one will ever find them.

Click-Through Rate: The Gatekeeper

When YouTube shows your thumbnail and title to a viewer (that's called an impression), what percentage of those viewers actually click? That's your CTR, and it's the first gate your video has to pass through. If people don't click, nothing else matters. Your content could be the best video ever made, but if the thumbnail doesn't stop the scroll and the title doesn't spark enough curiosity to earn a click, no one will ever know.

The average CTR across YouTube sits between 2% and 10%. For business and educational content, you want to aim for 4% to 8%. Above 8% is excellent. Below 4% means your thumbnail, your title, or both need work. We'll go deep on thumbnails and titles in Chapter 8, but for now, understand that CTR is the metric that opens the door to everything else.

What moves the needle on CTR? Clean, readable thumbnails with minimal text. Specific titles that promise clear value instead of vague curiosity. Faces showing genuine emotion (not the fake shock face every guru uses). Contrast and color that make your thumbnail pop in a sea of sameness.

Average View Duration: The Quality Signal

Of the people who click, how long do they actually watch? This is measured in absolute minutes and as a percentage of your total video length. Average View Duration is YouTube's primary signal for content quality. It's the algorithm asking, "Did this video deliver on the promise of its title and thumbnail?"

The average across all YouTube content is roughly 50% retention at the halfway point, and then it drops off. For educational content, top performers maintain around 42% average view duration overall. Anything above 50% retention is exceptional, and if you're hitting those numbers, YouTube is going to push your content hard.

Strong hooks in the first 30 seconds make a massive difference here. So do pattern interrupt every two to three minutes, visual changes, tone shifts, or new segments that re-engage the viewer's attention. Open loops that make viewers want to stick around for the payoff. And above all, actually delivering on whatever you promised in the title. It sounds obvious, but you'd be amazed how many creators bait the click and then wander off topic for 12 minutes. YouTube's algorithm catches that now, and it punishes it.

Watch Time: The Volume Play

Watch time is AVD multiplied by views. It's the total minutes of viewing your video accumulates across all viewers. YouTube weights this metric heavily because more watch time means more ad revenue and more platform engagement. Simple business math on YouTube's side.

This is where video length gets interesting, and where a lot of creators get confused.

A 15-minute video with 40% retention generates 6 minutes of watch time per viewer. A 3-minute video with 60% retention generates only 1.8 minutes. Even with lower retention as a percentage, the longer video produces more than three times the watch time. That's why the algorithm tends to favor longer content. Not because long is automatically better, but because the watch-time math almost always works in favor of depth.

This is exactly what we discovered with @VanLife. Three- to four-minute videos grew us by 300 to 400 subscribers per month. When we shifted to deeper content averaging around 18 minutes per video, growth jumped to 5,000+ subscribers per month. The accumulation of watch time triggered algorithmic amplification that shorter videos simply couldn't match.

Engagement Signals: The Trust Indicators

Likes, comments, shares, and saves all tell YouTube that viewers found genuine value in your content. But they're not all weighted equally.

Comments carry the most weight because they require real effort. Someone who takes the time to type a thoughtful comment is deeply engaged with your content, and YouTube knows that. Shares signal that the content is valuable enough to recommend to someone else, which is a powerful endorsement. Saves (adding to playlists or "Watch Later") indicate content worth returning to, which tells YouTube your video has lasting value. Likes are the weakest signal of the four, but they still contribute to the overall engagement picture.

Does that make sense? The harder it is for a viewer to do something, the more YouTube values that action as a signal. A comment beats a like. A share beats a comment. Build your content to earn the hard engagement, not just the easy clicks.

Session Continuation: The Platform Play

After watching your video, does the viewer keep watching more content on YouTube, or do they leave the platform? Videos that lead viewers into longer YouTube sessions get rewarded with more recommendations. This one is pure platform self-interest on YouTube's part, and smart creators use it to their advantage.

End screens that link to related videos help. Verbally suggesting a "watch next" video in the last 30 seconds helps. Creating content series that naturally flow into each other helps a lot. Playlists that autoplay through related topics keep people on the platform, and keep YouTube happy.

Think of it this way: every time a viewer finishes your video and watches another video on YouTube (yours or anyone else's), you get credit for extending their session. YouTube rewards you for being a gateway to more watching, not a dead end.

The Satisfaction Revolution

Now let me tell you what actually changed in 2026, and why it matters so much for business channels.

YouTube started measuring viewer satisfaction more directly. Before this update, a video could game the system with clickbait to get a high CTR, then retain viewers through manufactured tension or cheap curiosity hooks. The metrics looked great even when viewers felt manipulated or let down.

That doesn't work anymore.

YouTube now tracks patterns that indicate whether someone was actually glad they watched your video. Do they come back to your channel? That's loyalty, and loyalty indicates satisfaction. Do they watch similar content afterward? That means their interest was genuine, not manufactured. Do they engage positively in the comments, or complain about being misled? Do they share the video? No one shares content that disappointed them.

This shift devastated clickbait channels and boosted authority channels. When your content genuinely helps people, when they finish your video feeling informed, equipped, or like they just received real value, those satisfaction signals light up. The algorithm sees it and rewards you with more reach.

Your content actually helping people is now the single best algorithm strategy that exists.

The Three Traffic Sources

YouTube sends viewers to your content through three paths, and understanding each one helps you build a complete strategy.

Search traffic is viewers actively searching for topics and finding your video in the results. This is intent-driven traffic, the highest-converting kind, because these people already have a problem they're trying to solve. To win search traffic, use keywords naturally in your title, description, and spoken content. Answer specific questions. Target search terms with real volume and manageable competition.

Suggested and browse traffic is YouTube recommending your video on the homepage or after other videos. This is discovery traffic, where YouTube decides your content might interest a particular viewer based on their watch history and your video's performance signals. High-CTR thumbnails and strong AVD are what drive suggested traffic. If your video holds attention, YouTube will show it to more people.

External traffic is viewers arriving from outside YouTube, through social media posts, your website, email lists, or other platforms. YouTube actually values external traffic because it brings new users to the platform. Sharing new videos across your channels, embedding them in blog posts, and emailing your list when you publish all create an initial surge that can trigger algorithmic amplification.

For business channels, the ideal mix is heavy on search traffic (which captures intent-driven leads), supplemented by suggested traffic (which expands reach to new audiences). External traffic is your catalyst to kickstart the other two.

AI INTEGRATION

Your Algorithm Optimization Analyzer

Use this prompt to analyze your channel's algorithm performance and identify specific opportunities you're missing. If you haven't started yet, bookmark this for after you publish your first five videos.

PROMPT: Algorithm Optimization Analyzer

I need help analyzing my YouTube channel's algorithm performance. Here are my current metrics from my top five videos:

Video 1: [Title]

- CTR: [X]%
- Average View Duration: [X] min ([X]% of total)
- Views: [X]
- Video Length: [X] minutes

[Repeat for videos 2–5]

My channel averages:

- Overall CTR: [X]%
- Overall AVD: [X]%
- Primary traffic source: [Search/Suggested/External]

Please analyze:

1. How do my metrics compare to benchmarks for educational/business content?

2. What patterns do you see in my top-performing vs underperforming videos?

3. Is my video length optimized for watch time?

4. What's my biggest algorithm bottleneck right now?

5. Give me 3 specific actions to improve my algorithm performance in the next 30 days.

Run this analysis monthly. Your metrics will tell you exactly where the algorithm is rewarding you and where it's holding you back. Small improvements in CTR or AVD can trigger significant jumps in reach. This isn't guesswork. It's data.

CASE STUDY

The Algorithm Optimization That Doubled Impressions in 60 Days

One of my coaching clients, a real estate agent in Colorado, came to me with a mystery. He'd been posting consistently for six months. Decent content. Solid understanding of his niche. But his views had flatlined around 500 to 800 per video. The algorithm wasn't pushing him anywhere.

We pulled his analytics, and the problem jumped off the screen immediately. His CTR was 2.8%, and his average view duration was only 34% of video length. The algorithm was testing his videos by showing them to small audiences, but viewers weren't clicking, and the ones who did weren't staying. YouTube had essentially concluded his content wasn't satisfying viewers, so it stopped showing it to new people.

We made four changes.

First, we overhauled his thumbnails. They were text-heavy and cluttered, the kind where you can't tell what the video is about from the tiny mobile thumbnail. We simplified to a single clear image, his face showing genuine curiosity (not the fake shock face), and a maximum of three words of text. His CTR jumped from 2.8% to 6.1% within three weeks. Same content quality. Completely different packaging.

Second, we reconstructed his hooks. His videos started with 30-second intros explaining who he was and what his channel was about. That's a viewer killer. Nobody cares who you are until they care what you know. We cut straight to value: "Most people get this completely wrong about buying in [neighborhood], and it's costing them thousands." Retention at the 30-second mark improved from 68% to 89%.

Third, we added pattern interrupts. His videos were visually monotonous, same angle, same energy, same framing for 12 straight minutes. We broke that up with B-roll every 90 seconds, camera angle changes, and text graphics at key points. Overall AVD improved from 34% to 47%.

Fourth, we extended his video length. He'd been keeping everything to 8 to 10 minutes, thinking shorter was better (Myth #4 from Chapter 2 in action). We pushed to 15 to 18 minutes with significantly more depth. Watch time per video nearly doubled, even with similar retention percentages. The math we talked about earlier in this chapter, playing out in real time.

Within 60 days, his impressions doubled. Within 90 days, they tripled. Subscriber growth went from around 100 per month to over 400 per month. Same posting frequency. Same niche. Same creator. Different algorithm treatment because we optimized for what YouTube actually measures.

The algorithm isn't mysterious. It's a system with clear inputs and clear outputs. Improve the inputs, and the outputs follow every single time.

CRAZY SIMPLE ACTION

Your Algorithm Health Check

Open YouTube Studio right now and pull the metrics for your five most recent videos. If you don't have five yet, use whatever you have. If you haven't started, bookmark this page and come back after your first five uploads.

For each video, write down four numbers: CTR percentage, average view duration as a percentage, total video length in minutes, and total watch time in hours. Then calculate the average across all five.

Now score yourself against these benchmarks:

- If your average CTR is above 5%, you're winning the click game. Your focus should shift to retention and watch time. If it's below 4%, your thumbnails or titles are the bottleneck, and that's where you should put your energy this week.

- If your average view duration is above 45%, your content is keeping people engaged. Consider going longer on your next video to capitalize on that retention. If it's below 35%, viewers are leaving early, which means your hooks, pacing, or content structure needs work.

- If your average video length is under 8 minutes, you're almost certainly leaving watch time on the table. If it's over 15 minutes with solid retention, you're sitting in the algorithm's sweet spot.

- Write down your single biggest bottleneck. Is it CTR (people aren't clicking)? Is it AVD (people click but leave early)? Is it video length (your retention is great, but your videos are too short to accumulate meaningful watch time)? Pick one. Just one. And commit to fixing that specific problem in your next video.

The algorithm rewards clarity of purpose. Know your weak point. Attack it. Measure the results. That's how you turn the algorithm from something you fear into the most powerful marketing tool in your business.

In Chapter 4, we'll map your specific YouTube business model, how videos turn into leads, leads turn into clients, and clients turn into revenue for your unique situation. The algorithm gets your content seen. Chapter 4 makes sure it gets your phone ringing.

CHAPTER 4
Your YouTube Business Model

OPENING HOOK

I was on a coaching call with a financial advisor last year when he said something that stopped me cold.

"Aaron, I've got 3,000 subscribers. I'm posting twice a week. My analytics look decent. But I haven't made a single dollar from YouTube."

Three thousand subscribers. Six months of consistent uploads. And zero revenue. Not because the content was bad. Not because the algorithm was burying him. But because he had no business model behind his channel.

He was making videos. He was not making money.

That might sound like the same thing to someone who's never done this before, but it's not even close. A YouTube channel without a business model is a hobby. It might feel productive. You might get encouraging comments and a slow trickle of subscribers. But unless you've designed a system that turns viewers into leads and leads into clients, you're building a beautiful bridge to nowhere.

The financial advisor had 3,000 people who knew his name, trusted his expertise, and regularly watched his content. That's an incredibly valuable audience. But he had no call to action in his videos, no lead magnet in his description, no follow-up sequence, and no clear path from "I just watched this video" to "I want to hire this person." He was sitting on a gold mine and didn't even bring a shovel.

This chapter is the shovel.

THE FRAMEWORK

The Five YouTube Business Models

Not every business monetizes YouTube the same way. And trying to force your business into the wrong model is one of the fastest ways to waste six months of effort. I've identified five distinct business models that work on YouTube. While some overlap, you need to choose a primary model before you start creating content. Your content strategy, your calls to action, your video topics, and even your video length will all shift depending on which model you're building.

Model 1: Direct Lead Generation

This is the model I teach most often because it works for the widest range of businesses. You create content that attracts your ideal client, build trust through valuable information, and convert viewers into leads who contact you directly for your services. Real estate agents, mortgage lenders, insurance brokers, attorneys, coaches, consultants, contractors, and most service-based businesses fall into this category.

The mechanics are straightforward. Every video ends with a clear call to action driving viewers to a landing page, a phone number, or a booking link. Your video descriptions contain links to lead-capture forms. You create content around the specific questions your ideal clients are already asking, so the people who find you are pre-qualified by the search term itself.

Revenue potential here is directly tied to your client value. A real estate agent closing one deal per month from YouTube at an average commission of $12,000 is generating $144,000 per year from the channel. A consultant landing two new clients per quarter at $5,000 each is adding $40,000 annually. The math compounds as your content library grows and more videos are working simultaneously.

If you sell a service and your clients have meaningful lifetime value, this is probably your model. It's the one Marcus from Chapter 1 used to generate $387,000 from a single video, and it's the one I'll reference most throughout this book.

Model 2: Authority and Speaking

Some business owners don't need direct leads. They need positioning. YouTube becomes their stage, and the content becomes a living portfolio that proves they know what they're talking about.

This model works well for authors, speakers, thought leaders, and executives who want to build influence in their industry. The revenue doesn't come from individual client leads. It comes from speaking engagements, book deals, consulting contracts, board positions, and partnership opportunities that flow toward recognized experts.

The content strategy is different from direct lead generation. Instead of answering local search queries, you're creating thought leadership content that demonstrates deep expertise on broader topics, industry trends, contrarian perspectives, case studies from your work, and long-form analysis pieces. The videos don't need a "book a call" CTA. They need to position you as the person event organizers, publishers, and decision-makers think of first when they need an expert.

Revenue is harder to track directly because the opportunities that come your way don't always announce themselves as "I found you on YouTube." But when a conference organizer watches twelve of your videos before reaching out with a $15,000 speaking offer, YouTube was the engine, even if nobody says it out loud.

Model 3: Digital Products and Courses

If you've packaged your expertise into courses, templates, ebooks, software, or other digital products, YouTube becomes the world's best product demonstration platform. Every video is a sample of what your paid content delivers. And if the free content is genuinely helpful, buying the full product becomes an obvious next step for the viewer.

This model scales differently than services. You're not trading time for money. A course priced at $297 that sells to 500 people per year generates $148,500, and your videos keep selling it while you sleep. The key is creating free content that solves a real problem but naturally leads to a bigger, more comprehensive solution that lives behind a paywall.

The trap to avoid is giving away so much in your free content that people don't need your product. You want to be generous with the "what" and the "why" while reserving the detailed "how" for your paid offering. Show them the framework. Give them a win. Then say, "If you want the complete system with all the templates and step-by-step walkthroughs, it's right here."

Model 4: Affiliate and Partnership Revenue

This model works when your content naturally involves recommending products, tools, or services. You earn commissions when viewers purchase through your affiliate links, real estate agents recommending moving companies, tech reviewers linking to gear, fitness creators pointing to supplements, coaches recommending software.

I'll be straight with you: affiliate revenue alone rarely justifies a YouTube strategy for a serious business. The commissions are thin, and the volumes need to be substantial before the income becomes meaningful. Where this model shines is as a supplement to one of the other models. You're already making content about your expertise. Some of that content naturally references tools and products. Adding affiliate links to those recommendations is essentially free money on top of your primary revenue stream.

Don't build your entire strategy around affiliate revenue unless your niche specifically supports it (product reviews, comparison content, tech tutorials). For most business owners, it's a nice bonus, not the main event.

Model 5: Ad Revenue and Sponsorships

YouTube pays creators directly through the YouTube Partner Program once they hit 1,000 subscribers and 4,000 watch hours (or 10 million Shorts views). Brand sponsorships become available as your audience grows. For channels with significant viewership, this revenue can be substantial.

For business owners, this is almost never the primary model. AdSense revenue on a business channel with 5,000 subscribers might be $200 to $500 per month. That's nice coffee money, but it's a rounding error compared to what direct lead generation produces from the same audience. Sponsorships typically don't become meaningful until you're well past 10,000 subscribers and have proven, consistent viewership.

My advice? Treat ad revenue and sponsorships as things that eventually happen to your channel, not things you optimize for from day one. Build your lead generation system. Build your authority. The passive revenue catches up when you're not looking.

Choosing Your Primary Model

Most business owners reading this book should start with Model 1 (Direct Lead Generation) or a combination of Model 1 and Model 3 (if you have or plan to build digital products). The other models are valid, but they require either larger audiences (Model 5), different content strategies (Model 2), or work best as supplements (Model 4).

Does that make sense? Pick one. Build your content strategy around that model. You can add secondary revenue streams later, but trying to optimize for everything at once means you optimize for nothing.

The Lead Generation Machine: How Videos Become Revenue

Since most of you will be running Model 1 or a variation of it, let me break down exactly how a video becomes money in your bank account. This is the path every viewer walks, whether they know it or not.

Stage 1: Discovery. A potential client searches YouTube for something related to your expertise. "Best neighborhoods in Raleigh for families." "How to choose a financial advisor." "What to expect during a kitchen remodel." They find your video in the search results or suggestions and click.

Stage 2: Trust Building. They watch your video. If it's good, they feel like they just received free advice from someone who clearly knows what they're talking about. They might watch another video. And another. Every minute of content they consume deepens the relationship, and they haven't spoken to you once.

Stage 3: Conversion. In the video, you mention a free resource (a neighborhood guide, checklist, consultation call, market report). The link is in the description. They click it, land on your page, and give you their contact information in exchange for the resource. They are now a lead.

Stage 4: Follow-Up. Your email sequence or CRM kicks in. But this isn't a cold follow-up. This lead already knows your face, your voice, your expertise. When you call them, they pick up. When you email them, they open it. The entire sales conversation is different because they came to you pre-sold.

Stage 5: Client. They hire you. And because they arrived through a trust-based funnel instead of a cold ad or a random referral, they tend to be better clients. Higher value. Fewer objections. More referrals after the deal closes.

That's the machine. Video to viewer to lead to client. And every video you publish adds another entry point to this machine. By the time you have 50 videos working, you've got 50 employees generating leads around the clock.

AI INTEGRATION

Your Business Model Blueprint

Use this prompt to map out your specific YouTube business model with real numbers from your industry.

PROMPT: YouTube Business Model Blueprint

I'm a [YOUR PROFESSION] in [YOUR MARKET].

My primary YouTube business model is:

[Direct Lead Gen / Authority / Digital Products / Affiliate / Ad Revenue]

Here are my business specifics:

- Average client/transaction value: $[AMOUNT]

- Current close rate on warm leads: [X]%

- Monthly client capacity: [X] clients

- Current lead sources: [list them]

- Do I have a lead magnet or free resource? [Y/N]

- Do I have an email/CRM follow-up system? [Y/N]

Based on my model, help me build:

1. A viewer-to-client conversion funnel specific to my business

2. A recommended lead magnet that would appeal to my ideal YouTube viewer

3. A CTA script I can use at the end of my videos

4. Revenue projections for 6 months and 12 months based on one video per week

5. The three biggest gaps in my current setup that would prevent YouTube from generating revenue

This prompt will force you to think through the entire revenue path before you create a single video. Most creators skip this step and then wonder why their channel doesn't make money. Don't be most creators.

CASE STUDY

Sarah's Revenue Rebuild: From Views to Pipeline

Sarah (not her real name, at her request) is a real estate agent in a mid-sized Southern market. When she came to me, she had been posting YouTube videos for eight months. Her content was solid, good production quality, decent topics, and she had built a small but engaged audience of about 1,800 subscribers.

The problem? She had made exactly zero dollars from YouTube. Not a single lead. Not one client. Eight months of work with nothing to show for it on the revenue side.

When I looked at her channel, the issue was obvious within five minutes. Sarah was creating great content with no business model behind it. Her videos had no calls to action. Her descriptions contained a link to her website homepage (not a landing page, not a lead magnet, just the homepage). She had no email capture. No follow-up system. No way for an interested viewer to take the next step without hunting through her website for a phone number.

She was building trust with every video but giving viewers nowhere to go with that trust.

We rebuilt her system in two weeks.

First, we created a simple lead magnet: a neighborhood comparison guide for her market. A clean PDF with genuinely useful information that went deeper than her videos, and a clear path to "book a call with Sarah" on the last page.

Second, we built a dedicated landing page that did one thing and one thing only: capture a name, email, and phone number in exchange for the guide.

Third, we wrote a CTA script she could deliver naturally at the end of every video:

"I put together a free guide comparing the top 10 neighborhoods in [city], with real pricing, school ratings, and my honest take on each one. The link's in the description, grab it. And if you want to talk about what's right for your situation, my number's in there too."

Fourth, and this is the part most people skip, we set up a three-email follow-up sequence. Nothing aggressive. Just a welcome email with the guide, a second email two days later with a video she'd already made about her market, and a third email four days after that with a soft invitation to schedule a call. Simple. Automated. Running in the background indefinitely.

Within 30 days of implementing the system, Sarah generated 47 leads. Within 60 days, she had three clients under contract representing over $38,000 in commission. Same content. Same audience. Same subscriber count. The only thing that changed was the business model behind the videos.

By month six, her YouTube channel had generated over $140,000 in commission from a mix of buyer and seller leads. She told me, "I was sitting on a gold mine and didn't even know it." That's exactly what happens when you bolt a real business model onto a channel that already has trust built up.

CRAZY SIMPLE ACTION

Map Your Revenue Path

Before you move to Chapter 5, I need you to answer five questions. These will form the skeleton of your YouTube business model. Don't overthink them. Just answer honestly, and we'll refine as we go.

- **Which business model is your primary play?** Direct lead generation, authority building, digital products, affiliate revenue, or ad revenue? If you're a service-based business, the answer is almost certainly direct lead generation. Write it down and commit to it.

- **What is the single most valuable thing you could offer a YouTube viewer for free?** This is your lead magnet, a guide, a checklist, a calculator, a free consultation, a market report. It needs to be valuable enough that giving up an email address feels like a bargain. Write down your best idea right now.

- **Where will you send people?** You need a landing page, even if it's a simple one built in Canva or Google Sites. Write down what tool you'll use and commit to building it before you publish your next video.

- **What happens after they give you their information?** Map out a three-step follow-up. Email one delivers the lead magnet. Email two shares an additional resource (a video, a blog post, a case study). Email three makes a soft offer to connect. That's your starting sequence. Write the three subject lines right now.

- **What is your conversion target?** If YouTube generates 20 leads per month and you close 10% of warm leads, that's two new clients per month. At your average client value, what does that mean in annual revenue? Write that number down. Tape it next to the YouTube Hourly Rate from Chapter 1.

If you can answer these five questions, you have a business model. Not a perfect one. Not a final one. But a working model that turns viewers into revenue from day one. Most creators go months without ever building this foundation and then wonder why their channel doesn't make money. You're not going to make that mistake.

In Chapter 5, we're talking equipment. And before you start sweating over camera budgets, I'll save you the stress: you already own the most important piece of gear you need. It's in your pocket right now.

CHAPTER 5
The "Good Enough" Equipment Stack

OPENING HOOK

I need to tell you about the most successful YouTube channel I've ever helped build.

The creator shoots everything on a five-year-old iPhone. No external microphone. No lighting kit. No gimbal, no drone, no teleprompter. He edits in a free app, never shows his face on camera, and films in his car between appointments.

His channel has generated over 200,000 subscribers and multiple seven figures in business revenue.

I have another client who spent $12,000 on equipment before posting her first video: a professional camera, studio lights, acoustic panels, a wireless lapel mic, a motorized slider, and a 4K monitor for editing. Her setup looked like a news studio.

After two years, she had 847 subscribers and had never made a dollar.

The difference wasn't equipment. It was the trap equipment creates.

When you convince yourself you need better gear, you're actually doing something far more dangerous: you're giving yourself permission not to start. "I'll begin once I have the right camera." "I need to set up my studio first." "My audio isn't good enough yet."

These aren't preparation. They're procrastination wearing a productive mask.

The phone in your pocket right now is better than the equipment used to film most of the videos that built today's biggest YouTube empires. The first five years of YouTube were dominated by 480p webcams and built-in laptop microphones. The creators who won weren't the ones with the best equipment. They were the ones who actually posted.

This chapter is going to free you from the gear trap forever.

THE FRAMEWORK

The Hierarchy of What Actually Matters

Before we talk about specific equipment, you need to understand what viewers actually care about. And the answer surprises most people.

Content quality accounts for about 70% of viewer satisfaction. Is your video actually helpful? Does it solve a problem, answer a question, or provide genuine value? A brilliantly shot video with nothing useful to say will fail. A rough-looking video with genuinely valuable content will succeed. I've watched this play out hundreds of times across my coaching clients. Content is the whole game.

Audio quality accounts for about 20%. This is where people get it backward. Audio matters far more than video. Viewers will watch a slightly blurry video with clear audio all day long. But they will immediately click away from a crystal-clear 4K video with echo, background noise, or muffled speech. Bad audio is the fastest viewer killer on YouTube.

Video quality accounts for the remaining 10%: resolution, lighting, composition. These things matter, but far less than you think. Any modern smartphone shoots video that would have been considered broadcast quality ten years ago. "Good enough" video is easily achievable. Obsessing over marginal visual improvements is one of the most common traps I see.

Does that make sense? This hierarchy should shape every equipment decision you make. Spending $3,000 on a camera while using your phone's built-in mic is backward. Spending $100 on a decent microphone while filming on your phone is smart. Follow the hierarchy and you'll spend less money, get better results, and actually start creating instead of researching cameras for the next six weeks.

Tier 1: The "Start Today" Setup

Total investment: $0 to $150. And this tier is sufficient to build a six-figure YouTube business. Everything above this is optimization, not a requirement.

Your camera is your smartphone. Any iPhone from the 11 forward or any flagship Android from 2020 onward shoots 4K video that exceeds what 99% of viewers need. You already own a camera better than what YouTube was built on. Lock your focus and exposure before recording, clean the lens with your shirt (this solves most blurry phone footage), shoot in 4K at 30 fps, and keep the phone stable.

For audio, the wired earbuds that came with your phone have a surprisingly decent microphone. If you want a small upgrade, a $25 lavalier mic that plugs into your phone dramatically improves clarity. The Boya BY-M1 or similar options work well, and you can find them on Amazon in about 30 seconds.

Your lighting is a window. Natural light from a window is the most flattering light source available, and it costs nothing. Face the window, not away from it. If you need to film at night or in windowless spaces, a basic ring light for $25 to $50 provides even, soft lighting. Don't overthink this.

Grab a $15 to $30 phone tripod to keep your shot stable and free your hands. Shaky handheld footage looks amateur, and a tripod solves that completely.

For editing, CapCut is free and has become the standard for mobile editing. It's powerful, intuitive, and most of my clients use it for their first 20+ videos. For desktop editing, DaVinci Resolve is professional-grade software that costs nothing. Either one handles 95% of what you need.

I probably have four or five clients who grew channels to 200,000 to 300,000 subscribers where everything was shot on a phone with no microphone and no editing. The equipment doesn't matter. Read that again if you need to.

Tier 2: The Professional Polish

Total investment: $500 to $1,500. This is where you go once you've proven your content works and want to level up the production quality.

If you want to step up from your phone, Sony's ZV line was designed specifically for content creators. The ZV-1 or ZV-E10 runs $500 to $750 and gives you a flip-out screen, built-in stabilization, and excellent autofocus for solo creators. That said, plenty of my clients stay on their phones through Tier 2 and invest the camera budget in better audio and lighting instead. Both approaches work.

Audio is where your Tier 2 money makes the biggest difference. The Rode Wireless GO II ($250 to $300) gives you broadcast-quality wireless audio. Clip it to your collar and forget about it. The Shure MV7 ($250) is another excellent option for studio setups. Either one puts you in the top 5% of audio quality on YouTube, and that's not an exaggeration. Most creators have terrible audio because they sink their budget into cameras. You won't make that mistake because you read the hierarchy section and understand the priorities.

For lighting, a two-point softbox kit ($80 to $150) eliminates harsh shadows and creates a professional look regardless of the time of day. A key light and fill light give you control over your environment. Add a full-size tripod with a fluid head ($100 to $200), and you have a setup that looks and sounds better than 90% of business channels on the platform.

Tier 3: The Production Studio

Total investment: $3,000 to $7,000+. I need to be direct with you about this tier. If you haven't generated revenue from YouTube yet, Tier 3 is premature. This is for creators who have proven their concept, are scaling, and want production quality that matches their growing authority.

At this level, you're looking at full-frame or APS-C mirrorless cameras like the Sony A7 IV, Canon R6 II, or Sony FX30, all in the $1,800 to $2,500 range. These give you outstanding low-light performance, cinematic depth of field, and professional video features that will serve you for five to ten years.

Audio moves to shotgun mics like the Rode NTG series ($250 to $400) mounted on camera or boom, paired with an external recorder like the Zoom H6 ($350) for backup and greater control. Lighting becomes a full three-point LED panel system ($400 to $1,000) with key, fill, and backlight for complete environmental control.

But I want to be crystal clear about something: Tier 3 equipment without Tier 1 content skills is a waste of money. I would rather you film 100 videos on your phone with great content than 10 videos on a $2,500 camera with mediocre content. Master the content first. The equipment upgrade will be waiting for you when you're ready.

The Real Gear Secrets Nobody Talks About

Your smartphone camera is limited by the operator, not the hardware. Lock focus. Clean the lens. Find good light. Keep it stable. That's four things. Master those four, and your phone footage will look better than most people's DSLR footage, because most people buy expensive cameras and never learn how to use them properly.

Equipment shopping feels productive, but it is almost always a form of resistance. Steven Pressfield wrote about this. Resistance is the invisible force that stops us from doing creative work, and it disguises itself as "useful" activities. Researching cameras for three weeks feels like you're moving toward your goal. You're not. You're hiding from the thing that actually scares you: pressing record and putting yourself out there.

If you've spent more time researching microphones than researching what your audience actually searches for on YouTube, your priorities are upside down. Flip them.

When you eventually upgrade, do it based on diagnosed problems, not assumed ones. Film 20 videos on your phone first. Then review them critically. Is the audio genuinely holding you back? Is the lighting clearly problematic on camera? Upgrade to solve real, documented problems, not hypothetical ones you read about in a gear review.

And here's the secret that matters more than all the others combined. The equipment that matters most is the equipment that reduces friction. A complicated setup you avoid using is infinitely worse than a simple setup you use every day. If your filming process involves 45 minutes of setup time, you're going to find excuses to skip it. If your filming process involves pulling your phone out of your pocket and hitting record, you'll create content consistently. Consistency builds channels. Not cameras.

AI INTEGRATION

Your Equipment Recommendation Engine

Use this prompt to get customized equipment recommendations based on your specific situation, instead of guessing or getting lost in Amazon reviews for three hours.

PROMPT: YouTube Equipment Advisor

I'm starting a YouTube channel and need equipment recommendations based on my specific situation:

Content type: [Talking head / Property tours / Tutorials / Interviews / Mixed]

Primary filming location: [Home office / Various locations / Outdoors / Car]

Current equipment I already own: [list everything]

Budget for new equipment: $[AMOUNT]

Technical comfort level: [Beginner / Intermediate / Advanced]

Biggest concern: [Audio / Video / Lighting / Portability / Ease of use]

Based on this, recommend:

1. The essential equipment I need (and nothing more)

2. What I should skip entirely at this stage

3. The single most impactful upgrade for my money

4. Specific setup tips for my content type

5. A timeline for when to consider upgrading (based on milestones, not calendar dates)

Run this before you spend a dollar. It will save you from buying gear you don't need and point you toward the one or two purchases that actually move the needle for your specific situation.

CASE STUDY

The Phone-Only Empire

Let me go deeper on the creator I mentioned in the opening, because his story destroys every equipment excuse that exists.

He's a real estate investor and educator who started his channel in 2019. His initial setup was an iPhone 8 (already two generations old at the time), the earbuds that came in the box, and natural light from whatever room he happened to be in.

He never showed his face on camera. Most videos were screen recordings with voiceover, or footage of properties shot handheld while he narrated. His editing consisted of cutting out mistakes and adding a simple intro he made in Canva. By every "professional" standard, his production quality was terrible. The audio had room echo. The video was shaky. The graphics were basic.

But his content was exceptional. He explained complex real estate concepts in plain language. He shared real numbers from real deals, not theoretical examples. He answered the exact questions his target audience was typing into YouTube's search bar. And he posted consistently: two videos per week for three years straight. He never missed.

Today he has over 200,000 subscribers. Millions of dollars in course sales. A coaching program with a waitlist. All built on a foundation of phone footage and earbuds.

When I asked him why he never upgraded his equipment, his answer was perfect. "Every hour I spend messing with equipment is an hour I'm not helping people. My audience doesn't care about my camera. They care about solving their problems. The day production quality starts losing me viewers, I'll upgrade. That day hasn't come."

He eventually did upgrade, to an iPhone 12 and a $30 lapel mic. That's it. That's the equipment behind a seven-figure YouTube business.

I tell you this story not to say equipment doesn't matter at all. It does, eventually. But I tell it because if this creator can build a seven-figure business on an iPhone 8 and free earbuds, your equipment is not what's standing between you and results. What's standing between you and results are the 20 videos you haven't made yet.

CRAZY SIMPLE ACTION

Your 10-Minute Equipment Audit

This is the fastest action step in the book. Open your notes app and answer these questions right now.

- Do you own a smartphone made in the last five years? Do you own earbuds with a microphone? Do you have access to a window with natural light? Do you have anything to prop your phone up (a tripod, a stack of books, literally anything)? If the answer to all four is yes, you have everything you need to start. Full stop.

- Be brutally honest with yourself. Is equipment actually your bottleneck, or is it something else? If you have a phone, earbuds, and a window, then your real obstacle isn't gear. It might be not knowing what to create (we cover that in Part Two). It might be time management (Chapter 14). It might be fear of being on camera (we'll address that too). Name the real obstacle. Write it down. Equipment is almost never the honest answer.

- Write down your Minimum Viable Setup. What camera will you use? (Probably your phone.) What audio solution? (Probably your earbuds or a $25 lav mic.) What lighting? (Probably a window.) That's your setup. Don't add to it. Don't upgrade it. Not yet.

- Pick a date to film your first video. Not "sometime next week." A specific date. Write it down. Tell someone about it so there's accountability. The equipment you have is enough. The upgrade you need isn't a camera or a microphone. The upgrade you need is pressing record.

In Chapter 6, we'll set up your channel for maximum conversion. Because how your channel looks and functions when a viewer lands on it matters more than most creators realize. A great video that sends someone to a sloppy channel page is a missed opportunity, and we're not in the business of missing those.

CHAPTER 6
Channel Setup That Converts

OPENING HOOK

Your channel page is your storefront. And right now, it's probably costing you subscribers.

Here's what happens thousands of times per day across YouTube. Someone watches one of your videos. They like it. They're intrigued. They click on your channel name to learn more about you. And then they leave.

Not because your content is bad. Not because they weren't interested. But because your channel page failed to answer three questions that every visitor asks within five seconds of landing on it:

- What is this channel about?

- Is this person credible?

- What should I watch next?

If your banner, profile photo, description, and video organization don't answer those three questions almost instantly, visitors bounce. They never subscribe. They forget you exist. And every future video you create loses a potential fan before it ever gets a chance.

I've audited hundreds of business YouTube channels. The pattern is consistent and kind of painful to watch: channels with optimized pages convert visitors to subscribers at 3 to 5 times the rate of unoptimized channels. Same content quality. Dramatically different results. The only variable is what the visitor sees when they click through to the channel page.

The good news? Fixing this takes about an hour. You do it once, and it works for you forever.

THE FRAMEWORK

The Channel Conversion Stack

Your channel page has seven elements that determine whether a visitor subscribes or disappears. I'm going to walk you through each one, and I need you to remember a single principle the entire time: clever is the enemy of clear. Cute channel names, artsy banners, witty descriptions, all of that kills conversions. Clarity wins. Every time.

Your Channel Name

Your name should pass what I call the "radio test." If someone heard it spoken aloud on a podcast or at a networking event, could they search for it and actually find you? If the answer is no, the name doesn't work.

For business channels, you have two strong options. The first is your name plus your niche: "Sarah Martinez Real Estate" or "Mike Chen Coaching." The second is a brand name: "Denver Home Experts" or "Scale Your Practice." Personal names build trust faster but limit pivots. Brand names allow team expansion but require more effort to establish credibility. For most solopreneurs and small business owners, your name plus your niche is the stronger choice.

Stay away from generic names like "Real Estate Tips" that could belong to anyone. Avoid clever names that obscure your topic, like "The Closing Table," where a visitor has to guess what you're about. And skip names with random numbers or symbols, they look spammy and are impossible to remember.

Your Profile Photo

For personal brands, this is a professional headshot where you're looking directly at the camera, smiling, with good lighting and a clean background. Your profile photo appears next to every comment you make and every video you post. It's your digital handshake, and it needs to look like someone people would want to work with.

Shoot it at 800 by 800 pixels minimum. YouTube displays it small (98 by 98) but uses the larger file in various places. Your face should fill about 60% of the frame. Bright, even lighting. Solid or simple background. For brand channels, a clean logo that stays readable when it's shrunk to the size of a thumbnail.

The mistakes I see over and over are sunglasses (blocks human connection), group photos (which person are you?), photos that are clearly ten years old (breaks trust the second a viewer watches your video and you don't match), and no photo at all, which screams amateur louder than anything else you could do.

Your Channel Banner

This is prime real estate. It's the first thing visitors see, and it has about two seconds to communicate three things: who you help, what you help them with, and why they should trust you.

The formula is simple. "Helping [AUDIENCE] achieve [OUTCOME]" plus one credibility marker. Something like:

- "Helping First-Time Homebuyers Navigate Denver Real Estate | 15 Years Experience."

- "Business Coaching for Entrepreneurs Ready to Scale | 500+ Clients Served."

- "Marketing Strategies for Local Service Businesses | $10M+ Client Revenue Generated."

Clear, specific, and provable.

Technically, you design at 2560 by 1440 pixels. But here's the catch that trips up almost everyone: YouTube displays different portions of your banner on different devices. The safe zone, meaning the part that's visible on everything, including mobile, is only 1546 by 423 pixels in the center. If your key text sits outside that zone, half your visitors will never see it. Use Canva's YouTube banner template. It shows you exactly where the safe zones are. Keep text large, fonts simple, and contrast high.

Your Channel Description

Your About section serves two audiences: humans who are deciding whether to subscribe, and YouTube's search algorithm that's deciding whether to surface your channel. The first 150 characters matter most because they appear in search results and when your channel gets shared.

Structure it like this. Start with one sentence explaining what viewers get from your channel. Lead with value, not credentials. Follow with two to three sentences establishing why you're qualified: experience, results, credentials, but keep it brief. Nobody reads a paragraph of self-congratulation. Then state what types of videos you publish and how often. This sets expectations and tells new visitors what subscribing actually means. Finally, drop your calls to action: your lead magnet link, your booking page, your website. Include keywords naturally throughout because YouTube reads this section for search indexing.

An example:

"Learn how to buy your first home in Colorado without the stress or confusion. I'm Sarah Martinez, a Realtor with 15 years helping first-time buyers navigate the Denver market. I've closed 400+ transactions and helped clients save an average of $12,000 through smart negotiation. New videos every Tuesday and Thursday covering home buying tips, neighborhood guides, and market updates. Download my free First-Time Buyer Checklist: [link]. Schedule a free consultation: [link]."

Clear. Specific. Searchable. That description works for humans and for the algorithm simultaneously.

Your Channel Trailer

This plays automatically for non-subscribers who visit your page. Think of it as a 60 to 90 second commercial for your channel. Most creators either skip it entirely or make it so long and boring that it actually hurts their conversion rate.

Keep it tight. Open with your core promise in the first five seconds: "Want to buy your first home without overpaying?" Then introduce yourself and your credibility briefly, spending no more than 15 seconds on this. Show quick clips from your best content to give visitors a taste of what subscribing gets them. Close with a direct call to action: "Subscribe for new videos every week on [your topic]."

If you don't have a trailer yet, don't let that stop you. Pick your best-performing video and set it as the trailer temporarily. A strong existing video is infinitely better than an empty trailer slot. You can create a dedicated one later when you have enough content to pull clips from.

Featured Sections and Playlists

Without organization, visitors see a random wall of videos and have no idea where to start. That's overwhelming, and overwhelmed people leave. Your channel page should guide visitors to the right content based on where they are in their journey.

Your first section should be either "Popular Uploads" or a curated playlist of your absolute best content. First impressions matter, and you want visitors seeing your strongest work immediately. Second, create a "Start Here" playlist with your 5 to 10 best foundational videos. This is for brand new visitors who need an entry point. After that, build three to five topic-based playlists organized around your main content themes. For a real estate agent, that might be "Neighborhood Guides," "First-Time Buyer Tips," and "Market Updates." Put your most recent uploads last so returning visitors can easily find new content.

Playlist naming matters more than people think. "Denver Neighborhood Guides" is searchable. "My Favorite Places" is not. Every playlist name should answer the question, "What will I learn from these videos?" If the answer isn't immediately obvious from the title, rename it. And here's something most people don't realize: playlists themselves rank in YouTube search. A well-named playlist can become a traffic source all on its own, pulling in viewers who search for that exact topic and then watch three, four, five of your videos in a row. That's a session time goldmine.

Links and Contact Info

YouTube lets you add links to your channel page. Use them strategically because the first link gets the most clicks by a wide margin. That first slot should be your highest-value conversion point, which for most business owners is your lead magnet landing page or your booking link. Not your generic website homepage. Not your Instagram. The thing that generates leads.

After your lead magnet, add your booking or calendar link (for service businesses), your website, and your primary social platform. Four links are plenty. More than that, and you dilute the click-through on your most important one.

AI INTEGRATION

Your Channel Copy Generator

Use this prompt to generate optimized copy for every element of your channel page in one shot. Fill in the brackets and let AI do the heavy drafting. Then edit it to sound like you.

PROMPT: YouTube Channel Page Optimizer

Help me optimize my YouTube channel page for conversions. Here's my info:

- **Business/Niche:** [WHAT YOU DO]

- **Target audience:** [WHO YOU HELP]

- **Key transformation:** [WHAT OUTCOME YOU DELIVER]

- **Credibility markers:** [EXPERIENCE, RESULTS, CREDS]

- **Content types I create:** [VIDEO TOPICS/FORMATS]

- **Posting schedule:** [HOW OFTEN]

- **Lead magnet/offer:** [WHAT I WANT VIEWERS TO DO]

  Please generate:

1. Three channel name options (personal brand style)

2. Banner text (under 10 words, fits safe zone)

3. Full channel description (About section) optimized for search

4. Channel trailer script (60–90 seconds)

5. Five playlist names for my content categories

   Make everything clear and specific. Avoid jargon or cleverness.

This gives you a solid first draft in about three minutes. From there, rewrite anything that doesn't sound like you, tighten the language, and make sure every word earns its place.

CASE STUDY

The Channel Makeover That Tripled Subscriber Conversion

A mortgage broker came to me frustrated. "I'm getting views," he said, "but nobody subscribes. I've been stuck at 1,200 subscribers for six months even though my videos get 2,000 to 5,000 views each."

I pulled up his channel page, and the problems jumped off the screen. His channel name was his company name, which meant nothing to a stranger. His profile photo was the company logo instead of his face. His banner was a stock photo of a house with no text at all. His About section was three sentences copied directly from his website. He had zero playlists, just a wall of 47 videos in random order. And no channel trailer.

His channel was converting visitors to subscribers at about 0.8%. The benchmark for business channels is 2–4%. He was losing subscribers on every video simply because his channel page failed to answer those three critical questions: What is this about? Should I trust this person? What should I watch?

We spent 90 minutes rebuilding everything. Changed his channel name to his actual name plus "Mortgage Made Simple." Replaced the company logo with a professional headshot where he's smiling and looking directly at the camera. Designed a new banner that reads: "Demystifying Home Loans for First-Time Buyers | 2,000+ Families Helped." Rewrote his About section from scratch using the framework I just walked you through. Created five organized playlists: "Start Here," "First-Time Buyer Guide," "Credit Score Tips," "Loan Types Explained," and "Market Updates." And cut a 75-second trailer from clips of his best existing content.

Within 60 days, his subscriber conversion rate jumped to 2.7%. That's more than triple where he started. He went from gaining 40–50 subscribers per month to 150–200 subscribers per month. Same view counts. Same content quality. Same posting frequency. The only thing that changed was how his channel answered those three questions when a visitor showed up.

Ninety minutes of work. Triple the growth rate. And it only had to be done once.

Does that make sense? This is what I mean when I say some of the biggest wins in YouTube are the unglamorous foundational stuff nobody wants to talk about.

CRAZY SIMPLE ACTION

Your One-Hour Channel Makeover

Block one hour this week. Not "sometime soon." Put it on your calendar right now. Here's exactly what you're doing in that hour:

- Spend five minutes on your channel name. Does it pass the radio test? Can a stranger hear it and search for it? If your name doesn't clearly communicate who you help or what you teach, change it today. Your name plus your niche is the safest bet.

- Spend ten minutes on your profile photo. Upload a professional headshot where you're looking at the camera and smiling. If you don't have one, take one right now with your phone against a clean wall with window light. It doesn't need to be perfect. It needs to be you, looking approachable, at 800 by 800 pixels.

- Spend fifteen minutes on your banner. Open Canva, use their YouTube banner template, and write your "Helping [AUDIENCE] achieve [OUTCOME] | [CREDIBILITY MARKER]" text in the safe zone. Keep it under ten words. Test it on your phone to make sure it's readable.

- Spend fifteen minutes on your About section. Use the structure from this chapter: hook with viewer benefit, establish credibility in two sentences, state your content promise and schedule, and add your lead magnet and booking links. Write it, paste it, done.

- Spend fifteen minutes organizing your content. Create a "Start Here" playlist with your five to ten strongest videos. Create at least three topic-based playlists with searchable names. Set your best video as your channel trailer if you don't have a dedicated one. Arrange your featured sections so the best content is first.

When you're done, pull up your channel page on your phone and pretend you've never seen it before. Can you answer those three questions within five seconds? What is this about? Should I trust this person? What should I watch?

If the answer to all three is immediately clear, you've built a channel that converts. If any of them are fuzzy, tighten it up until they're not. This is one of those rare tasks that takes an hour once and pays dividends on every single video you publish from this point forward.

In Chapter 7, we're going to discover the topics your audience is actually searching for. Because a perfectly set-up channel means nothing if your videos aren't answering the questions people are typing into YouTube's search bar.

CHAPTER 7
Finding Topics Your Audience Actually Searches For

OPENING HOOK

She was crying on our coaching call.

"I've posted 67 videos," she said. *"Sixty-seven. And I have 340 subscribers. What am I doing wrong?"*

I pulled up her channel while she talked. Nice production. Good energy on camera. Clear audio. Solid thumbnails. Technically, she was doing everything right.

Then I looked at her video titles:

- "My Journey Into Real Estate"

- "Why I Love Being a Realtor"

- "Thoughts on This Week's Market"

- "A Fun Day at the Office"

- "My Favorite Coffee Spots in Town"

I stopped scrolling. *"Can I ask you something? How did you decide what to make videos about?"*

"I just… made videos about what I was thinking about that week."

There it was. The mistake that kills more YouTube channels than bad lighting, poor audio, and inconsistent posting combined. She was creating content nobody was searching for.

YouTube is a search engine. People type in questions and problems, and YouTube serves them answers. If your video isn't the answer to something someone is actually searching for, it sits in the void, invisible, gathering digital dust.

I asked her to do one thing: open YouTube in an incognito window and type *"first-time home buyer."* She watched as YouTube auto-suggested dozens of searches:

- "First time home buyer mistakes"

- "First time home buyer tips 2026"

- "First time home buyer programs"

- "How much house can I afford"

"These are things people are searching for right now," I said. *"Thousands of people. Every day. And none of your 67 videos answer any of them."*

Silence on the call. Then: *"Why didn't anyone tell me this?"*

I'm telling you now. The most beautifully produced video in the world is worthless if nobody's looking for it. This chapter will make sure you never waste another video on a topic nobody cares about.

THE FRAMEWORK

The Demand-First Content System

Stop thinking like a content creator. Start thinking like a librarian.

A librarian doesn't write books about whatever they find interesting. They stock books that patrons are looking for. Your job is the same: figure out what your audience is searching for, then create the best possible answer.

I use four methods to generate unlimited topic ideas, all validated by real search demand. These aren't theories, they're the exact methods I use for my own channels and every client I coach.

Method 1: The Alphabet Soup Technique

YouTube's search bar is a window into the minds of your audience. When you start typing, YouTube suggests completions based on actual searches people are making. This is real data. Not guesses. Not assumptions. Proof that people are looking for these exact topics.

Open YouTube in an incognito or private browser window so your personal history doesn't skew the results. Type your core topic, something like *"selling a house," "mortgage rates,"* or *"home inspection."* Screenshot or write down every suggestion that appears. Then add the letter "a" after your topic and watch new suggestions populate. Do the same with "b," then "c," all the way through the alphabet. After that, try variations: *"how to [topic]," "why [topic]," "what is [topic]," "best [topic]."*

Fifteen minutes of this generates **50 to 100 validated topic ideas**. I've had clients build six months of content from a single alphabet soup session. That's not an exaggeration. Once you see how many questions people are actually asking about your area of expertise, the problem flips from *"I don't know what to make videos about"* to *"I have too many ideas and need to prioritize."*

When I ran this for *"buying a house,"* the results included:

- "Buying a house for the first time"

- "Buying a house with bad credit"

- "Buying a house checklist"

- "Buying a house from family"

- "Buying a house in 2026"

Each one of those is a video. Each one has proven demand. Each one is something your target audience is actively searching for right now.

Method 2: Steal Your Competitors' Winners

Your competitors have already spent years testing what works. You can learn from their wins in ten minutes without creating a single video.

Find five channels in your niche with 10,000 to 100,000 subscribers. Big enough to have meaningful data, small enough to be realistic comparisons. Go to each channel, click on *Videos*, and sort by *Most Popular*. Study their top 10 videos. What topics keep showing up? What title formats perform? What patterns emerge across multiple channels?

You're not copying their videos. That's both lazy and ineffective. You're identifying proven demand. If five different real estate channels all have top-performing videos about *"first-time buyer mistakes,"* that topic clearly resonates with the audience. Your version will have your market, your stories, your expertise, and your personality. Same proven demand, completely different content.

Think of it like restaurants. Ten pizza places in the same city aren't copying each other. They've all identified that people want pizza. Each one brings their own recipe.

Pay special attention to videos that outperform a channel's average. If a channel typically gets 2,000 views per video but one video hit 40,000, that topic struck a nerve. Also look for topics that show up as winners across multiple competing channels, evergreen subjects not tied to specific news events, and videos with unusually high comment counts relative to views, which signals deep audience engagement.

Method 3: Mine Your Own Client Conversations

You have an unfair advantage over every YouTube guru giving generic advice. You talk to real clients every single day.

Every question a client asks is a video topic. Every confusion you clear up is content waiting to be created. Every objection you overcome is a video that could pre-handle that objection for future clients before they even contact you.

Start keeping a running note on your phone. I keep one called *"Video Ideas."* Every time a coaching client asks a question I haven't heard before, it goes on the list. Every time I explain something and see the lightbulb go on, it goes on the list. Every time someone emails me a question after a session, it goes on the list. Within a month, I have **30–40 ideas**, all from real people who represent my target audience.

The magic of this method is that these aren't just topics with search demand. They're topics that move people toward becoming clients. They answer the exact questions your future clients have before they're ready to hire you. A viewer who watches your video about the five biggest mistakes first-time buyers make is already further down the trust path than someone who just saw your ad. Does that make sense?

You're not just creating content. You're building a library of answers that **pre-educates and pre-qualifies your leads** before you ever speak to them.

Method 4: The "People Also Ask" Gold Mine

Google shows you exactly what people want to know about any topic. Search a subject and look for the *"People also ask"* box in the results.

Those expandable questions are pulled from real search behavior. Each question is a potential video topic.

The trick most people miss: when you click to expand one question, Google loads more related questions below it. You can generate **20+ topic ideas from a single search** by clicking through that box.

Beyond Google, mine the platforms where your audience hangs out:

- **Reddit** subreddits in your niche show which questions get asked repeatedly and which posts generate the most engagement.

- **Quora** surfaces questions with high follower counts, indicating widespread interest.

- **Facebook Groups** where your audience gathers reveal frustrations and knowledge gaps in real time. And here's a sneaky one: find popular books in your niche on **Amazon book reviews**, specifically three-star reviews, show exactly what questions the book didn't answer. Those gaps are your opportunities.

The Topic Validation Filter

Not every topic idea deserves a video. Before you invest time creating content, run potential topics through **five questions**.

First, is there proven demand? Does YouTube autocomplete suggest it? Do existing videos on this topic have views? If nobody is searching for it, creating a video about it is the same mistake our agent with 67 videos made.

Second, can you realistically rank for it? Look at the top results. Are they all from channels with millions of subscribers, or are there channels your size competing? If every result is from a massive creator, pick a more specific angle. *"Best neighborhoods in Austin"* might be too competitive, but *"Best neighborhoods in Austin for families with dogs"* could be wide open.

Third, and this is the one people skip: will viewers actually be potential clients? A viral topic that attracts the wrong audience does nothing for your business. Every video should attract people who might eventually hire you, buy from you, or engage with your services.

Fourth, do you have genuine expertise on this topic? Can you add real value? Do you have stories, data, or experience that make your take worth watching over anyone else's?

Fifth, will this topic still matter in a year? Evergreen content compounds over time. News commentary dies within days. Prioritize topics with long shelf lives, these are the videos that keep generating leads month after month.

A topic that passes all five questions is worth your best effort. A topic that fails questions three or four should be skipped, no matter how much search volume it has. Volume means nothing if the viewers aren't your people or you can't deliver real value.

I see this mistake constantly. An agent sees that *"celebrity homes tour"* gets massive search volume and thinks, *"I should make that video!"* But who's searching for celebrity homes? Bored teenagers, not people looking to buy a house. High volume, zero business value. Stay disciplined with the filter.

AI INTEGRATION

Your Topic Brainstorm Generator

Use this prompt to generate topic ideas, then validate them using the methods above. AI generates the ideas. YouTube autocomplete confirms the demand. Never skip the validation step.

PROMPT: YouTube Topic Idea Generator

Generate YouTube video topic ideas for my business:

- My business: [WHAT YOU DO]

- My ideal client: [WHO YOU HELP]

- My location/market: [IF RELEVANT]

- Problems I solve: [TOP 3 CLIENT PROBLEMS]

Generate **30 video topic ideas** in these categories:

- 10 *How to'* tutorials my audience would search for

- 10 *Mistakes to* avoid' or 'Problems' topics

- 5 'Comparison' topics (X vs Y, Which is better)

- 5 *What to* expect' or '*Process* explained' topics

Format each as a searchable title someone would actually type into YouTube's search bar. Avoid clever or vague titles. Include location-specific variations where relevant.

This gives you a starting list in about two minutes. But remember, AI is brainstorming, not validating. Take every idea it generates and check it against YouTube autocomplete before adding it to your content plan. If YouTube doesn't suggest it, real people probably aren't searching for it.

CASE STUDY

The Realtor Who Stopped Guessing

Let's return to the agent from the opening. After our call, she did something that changed her entire business: she stopped making content about herself and started making content about what her audience was searching for.

We spent 30 minutes doing alphabet soup research for her market, Phoenix, Arizona. She discovered searches she never would have guessed on her own:

- "Moving to Phoenix pros and cons"

- "Phoenix neighborhoods to avoid"

- "Cost of living Phoenix vs Los Angeles"

- "Buying a house in Phoenix first-time buyer"

- "Best places to live in Phoenix for families"

Her next video was titled *"Moving to Phoenix in 2026: Pros and Cons from a Local Realtor."* She used the exact search phrase people were already typing. Same camera. Same lighting. Same editing style. The only difference was the topic.

That single video got **8,400 views in its first 60 days**, more than her previous 67 videos combined. It generated **23 inquiries from people actively planning to relocate to Phoenix**. Not random viewers. People with moving dates, housing budgets, and real intent to buy.

She followed up with *"Phoenix Neighborhoods to Avoid (And Where to Look Instead)"* and *"Cost of Living: Phoenix vs California."* Both performed similarly. The pattern was unmistakable. When she made content nobody was searching for, nobody watched. When she made content answering real questions, the views, the leads, and the clients followed.

Six months later, she had **4,100 subscribers** (up from 340), and she'd closed **12 transactions directly from YouTube leads totaling $214,000 in commissions**. Same person. Same camera. Same market. The only change was making videos people were actually looking for.

"I wasted two years making content nobody wanted," she told me. *"If I'd known this from the start, I'd be so much further ahead."*

Now you know. Don't waste two years. Don't waste two months. The difference between a YouTube channel that generates leads and one that collects dust isn't production quality, posting frequency, or subscriber count. It's whether you're answering questions people are actually asking. Start with demand, and everything else gets easier.

CRAZY SIMPLE ACTION

The 30-Minute Topic Bank Builder

Block 30 minutes. No distractions. No phone notifications. When you're done, you'll have a month of validated video topics.

- **Spend 10 minutes on alphabet soup.** Open YouTube in incognito mode, type your main topic, and write down every autocomplete suggestion. Then add letters a through z and capture more. Your goal is at least **15 validated topic ideas** from this exercise alone.

- **Spend 10 minutes on competitor research.** Find three channels in your space. Sort their videos by *Most Popular*. Write down every winning topic you could cover with your own unique angle and expertise. Focus on topics that outperform their channel's average views.

- **Spend 5 minutes on client questions.** From memory, write down the ten most common questions your clients or customers ask you, the ones you answer so often you could do it in your sleep. Each of those is a video.

- **Spend 5 minutes picking your first four.** Review everything you wrote down. Run each potential topic through the validation filter: proven demand, realistic to rank, attracts the right audience, you have real expertise, and it's evergreen. Pick the four strongest topics. Write them down. Those are your next four videos.

Put a filming date next to video number one. Not *"soon."* Not *"next week probably."* A specific date. Write it on your calendar. You now have topics people are actively searching for. No more guessing. No more hoping. Just answer the questions your audience is already asking.

In Chapter 8, we'll turn these topics into **titles and thumbnails that demand clicks**. Getting found means nothing if nobody clicks. And the difference between a good title and a great one can be the difference between 500 views and 50,000.

CHAPTER 8
Titles and Thumbnails That Get Clicks

OPENING HOOK

I once watched a creator ruin a perfectly good video with a terrible title.

She had filmed an incredibly valuable piece of content, a detailed walkthrough of a home inspection, pointing out every red flag buyers should watch for. Eighteen minutes of pure expertise. As a real estate coach, I knew this content could generate leads for years.

Her title? *"Home Inspection Video."*

Her thumbnail? A blurry photo of the house's exterior with no text.

The video got 234 views in three months. She concluded that *"YouTube doesn't work"* and almost quit.

I asked her to try an experiment. We changed nothing about the video itself, same content, same length, same everything. We only changed the title and thumbnail.

New title: *"17 Red Flags Home Inspectors Find (That Sellers Try to Hide)"*

New thumbnail: Her face looking concerned, pointing at a crack in a foundation, with bold text reading *"HIDDEN DAMAGE?"*

Same video. Different packaging.

Within 60 days, that video crossed 12,000 views. More importantly, it generated 23 direct inquiries from home buyers who wanted to work with an agent who clearly knew what she was talking about.

Your title and thumbnail are not decorations. They are the marketing campaign for your video. YouTube can show your video to a million people, but if your title doesn't spark curiosity and your thumbnail doesn't stop the scroll, nobody clicks. And if nobody clicks, your video might as well not exist.

THE FRAMEWORK

The Anatomy of a Click-Worthy Title

A great YouTube title does three things at once: it promises a clear benefit, creates curiosity, and matches search intent. Miss any of these, and your click-through rate suffers.

The benefit piece is the most straightforward. Viewers want to know what's in it for them before they invest their time. Your title has to answer, *"Why should I watch this?"* Weak titles focus on the topic. Strong titles focus on the outcome.

- *"Kitchen Renovation Tips"* is weak because it's vague.

- *"How to Renovate Your Kitchen for $15K (Not $50K)"* is strong because it promises a specific result.

- *"Understanding Credit Scores"* is weak.

- *"Raise Your Credit Score 100 Points in 90 Days"* is strong.

See the pattern? Specificity signals value. Vagueness signals boredom.

The curiosity gap is where psychology kicks in. Humans have an almost compulsive need to close open loops. When we encounter incomplete information, our brains itch until we get resolution. Great titles exploit this by opening a loop that can only be closed by watching the video.

- Numbers and lists create curiosity because viewers need to know if they're making mistakes.

- Unexpected contrasts challenge assumptions: *"Why Expensive Homes Sell Slower Than Cheap Ones"* makes you think, *"Wait, that's backwards?"*

- Hidden information titles imply insider knowledge: *"What Realtors Won't Tell You About Closing Costs"*

- Implied story titles pull viewers in: *"I Lost $40K on My First Flip"*

But curiosity must be honest. If your title promises secrets but your video delivers only basic information, viewers feel cheated.

They'll leave, dislike, and never trust you again. The curiosity gap should be real, your video must genuinely deliver something worth the click.

Search intent matching is the third piece, and it's where Chapter 7's research pays off. Your title needs to include the words people actually search for. YouTube matches search queries to video titles, and if your video is about first-time home buying but your title doesn't include those words, you're invisible to the people looking for exactly what you offer.

Front-load your keyword. Put the most searchable phrase at the beginning of your title, not buried at the end. YouTube's algorithm weighs the first few words more heavily, and viewers scanning search results read left to right.

- *"First Time Home Buyer Tips"* hits harder at the front than tacked on at the end.

The formula that ties all three together: **keyword or topic + benefit or curiosity hook + specificity.**

- *"First Time Home Buyer Tips: 5 Mistakes That Cost You Thousands"* hits all three. The keyword is front-loaded, the curiosity hook is the mistakes, and the specificity is the number five and the consequence of thousands of dollars.

- *"Phoenix Housing Market 2026: Best Time to Buy or Wait?"* puts the search term first, creates urgency, and poses a question the viewer needs answered.

Title Formulas That Work

You don't need to reinvent the wheel. There are seven title structures work across industries, and you can adapt them to virtually any topic you cover.

1. **Number List:** *"9 Things to Check Before Signing a Lease"*, promises a concrete, finite amount of value.

2. **How-To:** *"How to Buy a House with Bad Credit"*, promises a transformation.

3. **Mistake Warning:** *"5 Mistakes First-Time Sellers Make That Cost Thousands"*, nobody wants to be the person making those mistakes.

4. **Versus Comparison:** *"FHA vs Conventional Loan: Which is Better for First-Time Buyers?"*, helps viewers make decisions.

5. **Insider Secret:** *"What Home Inspectors Actually Look For"*, implies access to information others don't have.

6. **Complete Guide:** *"Buying Your First Home: Complete Guide for Beginners (2026)"*, promises comprehensive coverage.

7. **Case Study:** *"How My Client Sold Their Home in 5 Days for $30K Over Asking"*, real results are irresistible.

Keep a swipe file on your phone of titles that make you click. Analyze what pulls you in and adapt those patterns for your content. Over time, writing great titles becomes instinct rather than effort.

Even then, always write at least three title options for every video. The first title you think of is almost never the best. Your third or fourth option, after pushing past the obvious, tends to be the winner.

Thumbnail Psychology

If your title is the headline, your thumbnail is the billboard. It must communicate value and emotion in a fraction of a second, because that's all the time you get as viewers scroll their feeds.

The single most important rule is a **clear focal point.** Your eye should be drawn to one thing immediately. Cluttered thumbnails with multiple competing elements get scrolled past. The best thumbnails have a single dominant subject, usually a face, a product, or a location, with everything else supporting that focus.

Human faces outperform everything else. Data from our @gotcoach testing confirmed that faces outperformed text-only thumbnails by 3x in click-through rate. But the expression matters enormously:

- Genuine curiosity for educational content.

- Appropriate concern for warning videos.

- Authentic enthusiasm for positive content.

For business channels, avoid the exaggerated *"YouTube face"* with open mouth and fake shock eyes. That works for entertainment channels targeting teens, but for business audiences, it destroys credibility. Your expression should be one you'd actually make in a professional conversation.

Contrast and readability are non-negotiable. Thumbnails are tiny, especially on mobile where most YouTube viewing happens. Use bold, simple fonts with a maximum of three to four words of text. High contrast between text and background. If viewers have to squint to read your thumbnail text on a phone, it's not working.

Bright backgrounds tend to outperform dark ones, and yellow or red elements grab attention faster than cooler tones. One test on @VanLife showed that switching from a dark background to a bright one on the same video increased CTR by 1.4 percentage points, a meaningful boost when getting 100,000 impressions per month.

Visual curiosity is the final piece. The best thumbnails raise a question that can only be answered by watching:

- A before-and-after comparison.

- An arrow pointing at something unusual.

- A reaction to something off-screen.

The thumbnail makes the viewer think, *"What's going on here?"* and the title answers, *"Click to find out."*

Build Thumbnails Before You Film

This is the process change that transformed my clients' CTR more than any design tip.

Most creators film their video first, then scramble to create a thumbnail afterward. That's backwards. If you decide on your thumbnail concept before filming, you can capture the right expressions and images during the shoot instead of trying to fake them later.

Spend a minute or two during filming taking 10–20 photos specifically for the thumbnail, different expressions, angles, and gestures. Then edit your best option in Canva using YouTube's 1280×720 template. Add minimal text that complements your title (don't duplicate it), and always test at actual size. Shrink your thumbnail to how it'll appear in search results and make sure it's still clear and compelling.

Develop a consistent visual style over time. Consistent fonts, colors, and layout help returning viewers recognize your videos in their feed before they even read the title. That brand recognition becomes a click advantage. When someone scrolls past 50 thumbnails and yours is instantly identifiable, you've built a shortcut to trust that no individual title can match.

AI INTEGRATION

Your Title and Thumbnail Generator

Use this prompt to generate multiple title options and thumbnail concepts for any video **before you film**.

PROMPT: YouTube Title & Thumbnail Generator

Help me create compelling titles and thumbnail concepts for my YouTube video.

- **Video topic:** [DESCRIBE YOUR VIDEO CONTENT]
- **Target keyword:** [MAIN SEARCH TERM TO RANK FOR]
- **Target audience:** [WHO IS THIS VIDEO FOR]
- **Main takeaway:** [THE #1 THING VIEWERS WILL LEARN]

Please generate:

1. Five title options using different formulas (number list, how-to, mistake warning, comparison, insider secret)

2. Rate each title's curiosity factor (1-10) and search optimization (1-10)

3. Three thumbnail concepts describing: the main image, facial expression, text overlay (3-4 words max), and color scheme

4. One contrarian title that challenges conventional wisdom

5. Which title/thumbnail combo works best for click-through AND audience trust

This is for a business channel. Avoid clickbait that damages credibility.

Run this for every video **before you film**. Having your title and thumbnail concept locked in beforehand means you'll capture the right images during the shoot, and your content will actually deliver on the title's promise.

CASE STUDY

The Repackaging Experiment

A mortgage broker in Texas came to me frustrated with inconsistent results. Some videos performed well, others tanked, and he couldn't figure out why.

"I'm covering the same topics as channels bigger than mine," he said. *"My content is just as good. But they get 50,000 views, and I get 2,000."*

We pulled up his highest- and lowest-performing videos side by side. The content quality was nearly identical. The difference was entirely in the packaging.

His worst performer had 847 views in six months. The title was *"Mortgage Rate Update December."* The thumbnail was a generic stock photo of a house with small rate numbers nobody could read on mobile.

Compare that to his best performer at 34,000 views. The title was *"Mortgage Rates Just Dropped: Should You Refinance NOW?"* The thumbnail showed his face looking surprised with a bold downward arrow and the text *"RATES DOWN!"*

Same type of content. Same creator. Same production quality. One title was a bland statement, and the other created urgency and posed a question the viewer needed answered. One thumbnail was forgettable stock imagery, and the other had a human face with clear emotion and text that demanded attention.

We spent an afternoon rebuilding the titles and thumbnails on his 15 worst-performing videos. We didn't touch the content, just the packaging. Within 90 days, average CTR on those videos climbed from 2.1% to 5.8%. The 15 videos went from a combined 12,000 views to over 67,000. Channel subscriber growth rate doubled. He received eight qualified mortgage inquiries directly attributed to the revived videos.

Think about that. Those videos already existed. They were already uploaded. Already indexed. The content was already good. All that potential was sitting there collecting dust because the titles were boring and the thumbnails were invisible.

Here's what he told me three months later:

"I used to spend 90% of my time on content and 10% on titles and thumbnails. Now I spend 70% on content and 30% on packaging. That shift doubled my results."

Does that make sense? The content hadn't changed. The algorithm hadn't changed. Good content just needed the packaging it deserved.

CRAZY SIMPLE ACTION

The Title and Thumbnail Audit

Open YouTube Studio and block 30 minutes. You're about to find easy wins hiding in your existing content.

- Sort your videos by click-through rate. Identify your top three and bottom three performers. Study what your winners have in common. Is it numbers in the title? Faces in the thumbnail? A specific emotional tone? Then look at your losers. What are they missing? Write down the one pattern that separates your best from your worst. That pattern is your formula going forward.

- Take your three lowest-CTR videos and rewrite their titles right now. Use the formulas from this chapter. Replace vague topics with specific promises. Add numbers where you can. Create a curiosity gap that your video actually closes. If those videos have thumbnail problems (no face, cluttered text, dark colors), redesign those too. This is the highest-ROI 30 minutes you'll spend all month because you're improving content that already exists.

- Before you film your next video, write three title options and design a thumbnail concept first. Not after. **Before.** Decide which title creates the strongest combination of benefit, curiosity, and search intent. Plan the thumbnail image you need to capture during filming. Then film the video knowing exactly what you're packaging and what promise you need to deliver on.

- Start a swipe file today. Every time you scroll YouTube and something makes you click, screenshot it. Titles that hook you. Thumbnails that stop your scroll. Study them. Reverse-engineer what worked on you. Within a month, you'll have a library of proven patterns you can adapt for your own content.

Your title and thumbnail are the packaging. Great content in bad packaging stays on the shelf. And here's what most creators miss: this is the one skill that retroactively improves every video you've already published. You can go back right now and give your best content a second life. Give your videos the chance they deserve.

In Chapter 9, we'll master the **first 30 seconds** of your video, the hook that keeps viewers watching after they click. Getting the click is only half the battle. Keeping attention is where the real game begins.

CHAPTER 9
The First 30 Seconds: Hooks That Keep Viewers Watching

OPENING HOOK

You've won the click. Someone saw your thumbnail, read your title, and decided your video was worth their time. They're on your video now, ready to watch.

And then you lose them in eight seconds.

This happens constantly. YouTube's internal data shows that the average viewer decides whether to keep watching or click away within the first 10 to 15 seconds. Some research suggests it happens even faster, as quickly as 5 to 8 seconds for viewers who are casually browsing.

Think about your own behavior. How many times have you clicked on a video, heard "Hey guys, welcome back to my channel, don't forget to like and subscribe," and immediately clicked away? How many times has a video started with a 30-second animated intro, and you've already moved on before the actual content began?

Your opening isn't a formality. It's not a greeting. It's not a place to remind people to subscribe. Your opening is an audition. Every second, your viewer is subconsciously asking: "Is this worth my time?" Your hook must answer that question with a resounding yes before they even finish asking it.

I learned this lesson painfully on my @VanLife channel. Early videos had decent thumbnails and titles. People were clicking. But my retention graphs looked like ski slopes. Seventy percent of viewers were gone within the first minute. The problem wasn't my content. It was that I was burying my content under generic openings that gave viewers no reason to stay.

When I restructured my openings, when I started treating the first 30 seconds as the most important part of the entire video, everything changed. Average view duration climbed. The algorithm started pushing my content harder. Videos that would have gotten 5,000 views started getting 50,000.

Same content. Same production quality. Same topics. The only difference was what happened in the first half-minute.

THE FRAMEWORK

Why the First 30 Seconds Determine Everything

YouTube's algorithm is obsessed with viewer satisfaction. The earliest indicator of satisfaction is whether viewers stick around after clicking.

When someone clicks your video and leaves within 10 seconds, YouTube interprets that as a signal that your video didn't deliver what the title and thumbnail promised. Do this enough times, and YouTube stops showing your videos to new viewers. Why would it recommend content that people immediately abandon?

The flip side is powerful. When viewers click and stay, past the first 30 seconds, the first minute, and deeper into the video, YouTube sees proof that your content is worth recommending. The algorithm rewards you with more impressions, more suggested placements, more reach. Strong openings lead to better retention. Better retention leads to more promotion. More promotion leads to more views. It's a flywheel, and your hook is what sets it spinning.

Pull up the audience retention graph for any of your videos in YouTube Studio. You'll almost certainly see a steep drop in the first 30 seconds. That's the retention cliff, the point where casual viewers decide to leave. Your job is to make that cliff as shallow as possible by giving viewers an immediate reason to stay.

The Five Opening Sins

Before I show you what works, let me kill what doesn't. These opening mistakes destroy retention instantly, and I see every single one of them when I audit business channels:

1. **The Generic Greeting** – "Hey guys, welcome back to my channel!" Tells viewers nothing. Doesn't promise value. Doesn't create curiosity. It's wasted breath that gives viewers time to click

away. Your regular viewers don't need a greeting. They're already here. New viewers don't care about greetings. They want to know if the video is worth watching.

2. **The Subscribe Beg** – "Before we get started, make sure to smash that like button and subscribe!" You're asking viewers to commit before you've proven any value. It's like asking someone to marry you on the first date. Earn the subscription by delivering great content first. Ask for it later. Or not at all.

3. **The Long Intro Animation** – Animated logo sequences, dramatic music builds, fancy graphics. They might look professional, but they're viewer repellent. Every second of intro animation is a second where viewers can leave. If you must have a branded intro, keep it under three seconds and place it after your hook, not before.

4. **The Slow Wind-Up** – "So today I wanted to talk about something that I've been thinking about for a while, and I think it's really important, so let me just give you some background first..." By the time you get to the point, half your audience is gone. Get to the value immediately. Context can come later.

5. **The Apology Opening** – "Sorry I haven't posted in a while" or "I know the lighting isn't great in this one." Never open with weakness. Viewers don't care about your posting schedule or production challenges. They care about whether you can help them. Lead with strength.

Eight Hook Formulas That Work

Every great YouTube opening uses one of these proven structures. I use all eight across my own channels, and I've taught them to hundreds of coaching clients. Match the formula to your content type:

1. **Problem-Agitate-Promise** – State a problem your viewer has, agitate it by highlighting the consequences, then promise a solution. *If you're a first-time home buyer, you're probably making at least one of these five mistakes, and any single one of them could cost you tens of thousands of dollars. By the end of this video, you'll know exactly what to*

avoid and how to protect yourself." Best for educational content, how-to videos, and mistake-focused content.

2. **Shocking Statement** – Open with a counterintuitive claim that challenges what viewers believe. *"The 20% down payment rule is a myth, and following it might actually be costing you money. Let me show you why."* When something contradicts a viewer's assumption, their brain demands resolution. They have to keep watching. Use this. Best for myth-busting content, contrarian takes, and industry secrets.

3. **Result Tease** – Show the end result first, then promise to reveal how. *"This house sold in three days for $40,000 over asking price. I'm going to show you exactly what the sellers did to make that happen, and you can do the same thing."* Results are irresistible. When viewers see proof that something works, they'll stick around to learn the method. Perfect for case studies and transformation content.

4. **Story Hook** – Pull viewers in emotionally from the first sentence. *"Last month, I got a call from a client in tears. She'd just found out her dream home had a $60,000 foundation problem that the seller had hidden. What I told her next saved her from the biggest mistake of her life."* Humans are wired for stories. An unfinished story creates an open loop that viewers need to close by watching. Best for client stories, personal experiences, and cautionary tales.

5. **Direct Question** – Ask what your viewer is already asking themselves. *"Should you buy a house right now, or wait for prices to drop? I'm going to give you the honest answer, and it's probably not what you're expecting."* Signals the video was made for them and adds a curiosity gap they can't resist. Best for FAQ content, decision-focused videos, and timely topics.

6. **Preview Stack** – Tell viewers exactly what they'll learn, stacking multiple value promises in rapid succession. *"In the next 12 minutes, you're going to learn the three neighborhoods where prices are still undervalued, the one type of property that's actually appreciating right now, and the exact script I use to negotiate $20,000 off any home."* Works because each promise adds another reason to stay. Best for list videos, comprehensive guides, and value-packed content.

7. **Proof Hook** – Lead with credentials that establish immediate credibility. *"I've helped over 400 families buy their first home, and I see the same three mistakes over and over. Here's what they are, and more importantly, how to avoid them."* When the topic requires trust (financial advice, legal guidance, medical information), front-loading your authority gives viewers permission to listen. Best for expert advice and trust-dependent topics.

8. **Cold Open** – Start with the most exciting moment from later in the video, then cut to your intro. You show a clip of yourself walking through a house and saying, *"See this crack right here? This is a $50,000 problem that the seller didn't disclose, and I'm going to show you how to spot things like this before you buy."* Then transition to your regular opening. Borrows a technique from television and film, and it works incredibly well for property tours, walkthroughs, and reveal-style content.

The 30-Second Structure

Now that you have the formulas, here's exactly how to structure your opening half-minute so that every element earns its place.

The first five seconds are your **hook**. Your strongest opening line from the formulas above. No throat-clearing, greetings, or preamble. The very first words out of your mouth should either deliver value or spark curiosity so strong the viewer can't leave.

Seconds five through fifteen are your **promise**. Expand on what viewers will get from watching. Be specific about the value. Create an open loop that can only be closed by watching the rest of the video. This is where you answer the viewer's unspoken question: "What's in it for me if I keep watching?"

Seconds fifteen through twenty-five are your **credibility**. One sentence establishing why you're qualified to deliver on the promise. This doesn't need to be a full bio. "After 15 years in this market" or "Having helped 300 clients through this exact situation" is enough. Viewers don't need your life story, they need a reason to trust your advice.

The last five seconds are your **transition** into the main content. This is where a brief branded intro can go, if you have one (under three seconds), or simply a bridge like "Here's what you need to know." By this point, viewers have every reason to stay: they know what they'll learn, they trust you to teach it, and the good stuff is about to start.

AI INTEGRATION

Your Hook Script Generator

Use this prompt to generate multiple hook options for any video before you film. Having five options to choose from means you pick the strongest one, not just the first one you think of.

PROMPT: YouTube Hook Generator

Help me create compelling opening hooks for my YouTube video.

- **Video topic:** [WHAT THE VIDEO IS ABOUT]

- **Main value delivered:** [WHAT VIEWERS WILL LEARN]

- **Target viewer's problem:** [WHAT PAIN POINT THIS SOLVES]

- **My credibility:** [EXPERIENCE/RESULTS]

- **Video style:** [Educational/Story/Tour/Review]

Please generate:

1. A **Problem-Agitate-Promise** hook (3–4 sentences)

2. A **Shocking Statement** hook (2–3 sentences)

3. A **Story hook opening** (3–4 sentences)

4. A **Direct Question** hook (2–3 sentences)

A **Preview Stack** hook listing 3 specific things they'll learn

For each hook, also provide:

- A one-sentence credibility statement to follow

- A transition line into the main content

Make each hook conversational and natural. Not salesy or over-hyped, these should sound like something a trusted expert would actually say.

Generate hooks **before** you film, not after. When you know your hook in advance, you can deliver it with confidence and energy. Trying to write a hook in post-production, stuck with whatever you happened to say at the beginning, rarely works as well.

CASE STUDY

The Retention Transformation

Daniel Kotula, the consultant from Prague we met in Chapter 2, had a hook problem he didn't even know about.

After we fixed his overall strategy, switching from entertainment tactics to authority positioning, his videos were getting better click-through rates. People were finding his content. But his average view duration was stuck at 35%, well below the benchmark for educational content.

When we analyzed his retention graphs, the pattern was obvious. Every single video showed a massive drop in the first 30 seconds. He was losing 40–50% of viewers before he even got to the valuable content.

The culprit was his standard opening:

"Hey everyone, welcome back to my channel. If you're new here, my name is Daniel, I'm a real estate agent based in Prague, and on this channel I talk about everything related to buying and selling property in the Czech Republic. Make sure to subscribe if you haven't already. Okay, so today we're going to talk about…"

Thirty-two seconds. Thirty-two seconds of zero value before he got to the point. By the time he said something useful, half his audience was already gone.

We rebuilt his opening structure completely. His new approach:

"If you're buying property in Prague right now, there's one neighborhood that's completely undervalued, and most buyers don't even know it exists. I've sold 15 properties there in the last year, and my clients are seeing 20% appreciation while the rest of the market is flat. I'm going to show you exactly where it is and why the numbers make sense."

Same creator. Same expertise. Same production quality. Different structure.

Over the next 90 days, his average view duration climbed from 35% to 52%. His 30-second retention improved from 55% to 78%, meaning he went from losing almost half his viewers immediately to keeping more than three-quarters of them. YouTube started recommending his videos three times more frequently because the retention signals told the algorithm his content was satisfying viewers. Subscriber growth accelerated from 400 per month to 1,200 per month. And the lead quality improved because viewers who stayed longer arrived more educated and more ready to work with him.

The improvement in 30-second retention cascaded through everything. When more viewers stayed past the opening, more of them watched the whole video. When more people watched the whole video, YouTube promoted it more. When YouTube promoted it more, more potential clients discovered his channel. All of that from changing the first 30 seconds.

"I spent months trying to improve my content, my editing, my thumbnails," Daniel told me later. "The biggest improvement came from changing how I started my videos. I wish I'd done it sooner."

CRAZY SIMPLE ACTION

The Hook Audit and Rebuild

Block 30 minutes. You're going to diagnose your current hook problem and fix it before your next video.

1. Pull up the retention graphs for your three most recent videos in YouTube Studio. For each one, write down the percentage of viewers remaining at the 30-second mark. If you're above 70%, your hooks are working. If you're below 60%, your openings are costing you viewers and everything that follows in this chapter applies immediately. Watch the first 30 seconds of each video as if you were a stranger. Are you committing any of the five opening sins? Generic greeting, subscribe beg, long intro animation, slow wind-up, or apology opening? Be ruthless with yourself.

2. Pick the hook formula that best fits your most common video type. For most business channels, the **Problem-Agitate-Promise** or the **Direct Question** will be your go-to. Write a template opening using that formula with your specific niche, credibility markers, and typical value proposition. This becomes your default structure. You'll customize it for each video, but the bones stay the same.

3. Write the hook for your next video right now. Fill in the 30-second structure: your hook line (0–5 seconds), your value promise (5–15 seconds), your credibility statement (15–25 seconds), and your transition (25–30 seconds). Read it out loud three times. Time yourself. Does it fit in 30 seconds? Does it sound natural when spoken? Tighten it until it flows and lands with energy.

4. Make this commitment: from this point forward, every video you create uses this structure. Your first words will always deliver value or create curiosity. No more generic greetings. No more slow wind-ups. No more giving viewers a reason to leave. Hook them in the first five seconds, and they'll stay for the whole video.

Your hook isn't just the start of your video, it's the foundation everything else builds on. Master the first 30 seconds, and the rest of the video has a fighting chance.

In Chapter 10, we'll structure the rest of your video for maximum retention, because keeping viewers hooked for 10 or 15 minutes requires more than just a great opening.

CHAPTER 10
Structuring Videos for Maximum Retention

OPENING HOOK

You've nailed your hook. Viewers are staying past the first 30 seconds. Your retention cliff has become a gentle slope.

And then something happens around the three-minute mark.

The graph starts sagging. Viewers who survived your opening begin trickling away. By the midpoint of your video, you've lost another 30%. By the end, you're down to a fraction of who started.

This is the "sagging middle" problem, and it plagues nearly every creator who hasn't learned to structure their content strategically.

Your viewers aren't leaving because they're bored with your topic. They're leaving because their brain needs a reason to stay engaged. Without deliberate structure, your video becomes a monotonous stream of information that the brain tunes out the same way it tunes out background noise.

I discovered this the hard way on @VanLife. My short videos had decent retention throughout. But when I pushed to 10, 15, even 20 minutes, chasing that watch time the algorithm rewards, my retention graphs looked like playground slides. Great start, then a steady decline all the way down.

The problem wasn't that I was saying too much. It was that I was saying it wrong. I was treating a 15-minute video like a 15-minute monologue instead of what it actually needs to be: a series of connected moments, each giving viewers a fresh reason to keep watching.

When I learned to structure videos properly, to create what I call "retention architecture," everything changed. Average view duration climbed. The algorithm pushed harder. Videos that would have gotten 10,000 views started getting 100,000.

The insight that transformed my approach was simple: Viewers don't watch videos. They watch moments. Your job isn't to fill time. It's to create a sequence of moments that are each individually compelling, while building toward a satisfying conclusion.

THE FRAMEWORK

The Psychology of Why Viewers Leave

Viewers don't leave randomly. They leave at predictable moments for predictable reasons. Understanding these exit triggers is the first step to preventing them.

- **Promise fulfilled too early:** If your title promised "3 Tips for First-Time Buyers" and you've delivered all three tips by minute four of a twelve-minute video, viewers have no reason to stay. They got what they came for. The fix isn't to pad your content. It's to structure your promise so the most valuable part comes later, or stack multiple promises throughout the video.

- **Cognitive overload:** When you deliver dense information without breaks, viewers' brains get tired. They're not consciously thinking "this is too much." They just feel the urge to click away. The fix is deliberate pacing: intense information followed by lighter moments, stories, or visual changes that let the brain rest while still engaged.

- **Predictability:** Predictability kills retention just as surely as bad content. The brain is a prediction machine, and when it can predict what's coming next, it loses interest. If your video settles into the same energy, same visuals, same pacing for twelve straight minutes, the brain checks out. The fix is pattern interrupts, which I'll cover shortly.

- **Absence of open loops:** An open loop is an unresolved question or tension. When you close all your loops as you go, there's nothing pulling viewers forward. But when you strategically leave loops open, saying something like "I'll show you exactly how this works in a moment," viewers stay to see the resolution. Smart creators open new loops before closing old ones, creating a constant pull toward the next section.

- **Lack of stakes:** If viewers don't feel like they'll miss something important by leaving, they'll leave. You need to establish and reinforce stakes throughout: reminding viewers why this matters, what they'll gain by staying, what they'll miss by going.

Pattern Interrupts: The Retention Reset Button

A pattern interrupt is anything that breaks the expected flow and recaptures attention. Think of it as a mini-hook within your video, a moment that makes the viewer's brain perk up and re-engage.

- **Visual interrupts:** Camera angle changes from wide to close-up, B-roll footage that cuts away from the talking head, on-screen graphics and text overlays, location changes (even just moving to a different spot), and screen recordings or demonstrations. Every visual change gives the viewer's brain a fresh stimulus to process, buying you another stretch of attention.

- **Audio interrupts:** Music changes or well-placed sound effects, shifts in your speaking pace and energy, strategic pauses that create emphasis, and transitions between voice-over segments and on-camera delivery. Your voice alone can create pattern interrupts if you vary its rhythm, volume, and intensity throughout the video.

- **Content interrupts:** An unexpected statement or contrarian take stops viewers mid-scroll. A story that breaks up instructional content gives the brain a narrative to follow. A direct question to the viewer creates momentary engagement. Humor or personality moments humanize the content. And the classic "But here's the thing..." pivot signals that something unexpected is about to happen.

Rule of thumb: Include some form of pattern interrupt every 60 to 90 seconds. This doesn't mean chaotic editing. It means deliberate variation that keeps the brain engaged without being exhausting.

Four Video Structures That Work

Different content types call for different structural approaches. Here are four frameworks that work consistently for business channels:

1. **The Countdown:** Ideal for list videos. Present items in ascending order of importance, with the best saved for last. This creates natural anticipation because viewers don't want to miss the number-one item. Tease the value of your top pick without

revealing it in the hook. Build momentum through items five through three. Make item two strong enough that viewers think, "If this is only number two, what's number one?" Then deliver your payoff. Number your items on screen so viewers can track their progress. When someone sees "#3" they know there's still a #2 and #1 coming, which keeps them watching.

2. **Problem-Solution:** Works best for how-to content. Establish a painful problem, agitate it by highlighting the consequences, then systematically solve it. The deeper you make the viewer feel the problem, the more they need to stay for the solution. Most creators rush through the agitation phase, don't. Spend more time there than feels comfortable. Show why this problem is serious, costly, or painful. Walk through what doesn't work and why. Then deliver your method step by step, followed by proof that it works. The agitation is where you earn the viewer's investment in the solution.

3. **Story Arc:** Designed for case studies, tours, and transformation content. Follow a narrative structure with setup, rising action, climax, and resolution. Humans are hardwired for stories. We literally cannot help but stay to see how they end. For property tours, the "story" is the journey through the home. Create narrative tension: "Now let's see if the master bedroom lives up to what the rest of the house promised." For case studies, the story is the transformation: where the client started, what went wrong, the turning point, and the outcome.

4. **Tutorial:** For step-by-step instructional content. Walk through a process from start to finish, but the key is chunking: breaking the process into clear stages with progress markers. Show the end result first to create desire, then briefly list all steps (giving viewers a roadmap of what's coming), then walk through each step clearly numbered and demonstrated. Close with common mistakes to avoid, which adds value beyond the basic instruction. Use on-screen chapter markers and step numbers throughout. Viewers love knowing exactly where they are in the process, and it makes your video more searchable.

Strategic Value Placement

One mistake creators make is front-loading all their best content. They deliver their biggest insight at minute two, then spend the next ten minutes on increasingly less valuable information. Retention craters because viewers got what they needed early.

The better approach is what I call **value peaks**. Distribute your most compelling content at strategic intervals throughout the video. Your opening is **Peak 1**, the strong hook that promises value. At around the 25% mark, deliver **Peak 2**, your first major insight or revelation. At the halfway point, hit **Peak 3** with a surprising fact, story, or pivot. At the 75% mark, deliver **Peak 4**, which should be your most valuable or actionable content. Then close with **Peak 5**, a strong conclusion with clear next steps.

Between peaks, you deliver supporting content: context, examples, demonstrations. But the peaks keep pulling viewers forward. They just experienced something valuable and sense more is coming. At each peak, briefly tease what's next: "That tip alone could save you thousands, but the next one is even more important." This creates forward momentum that carries viewers through the supporting content and into the next payoff.

AI INTEGRATION

Your Video Structure Architect

Use this prompt to create a retention-focused structure for any video before you script or film.

PROMPT: YouTube Video Structure Generator

Help me structure my YouTube video for maximum retention.

- **Video topic:** [WHAT THE VIDEO COVERS]

- **Target length:** [X MINUTES]

- **Content type:** [List / How-To / Case Study / Tour]

- **Main points to cover:** [LIST YOUR KEY POINTS]

- **Best insight/tip:** [YOUR MOST VALUABLE POINT]

Please create:

1. A complete video outline with timestamps

2. Identify where to place 5 value peaks throughout the video

3. Suggest 6-8 specific pattern interrupts with timestamps (visual changes, B-roll, tone shifts)

4. Write 3 open loop statements to use at strategic points that tease upcoming content

5. Identify potential drop-off danger zones and how to address them

6. Suggest where to place a mid-video CTA that does not feel forced

Structure this so the most valuable content comes at strategic intervals, not all at the beginning. Run this before scripting or filming. Having a clear retention-focused structure in advance makes filming easier and ensures you capture all the B-roll and visual elements you'll need for pattern interrupts.

CASE STUDY

From Sagging Middle to Sustained Engagement

A real estate coach in my program, Jennifer, was creating solid 15-minute market update videos. Her hooks were strong (we'd already fixed that in a previous session), but her retention graphs still showed a steady downward slope after the first two minutes.

"People are clicking, they're staying for the intro, but then they just slowly bleed out," she told me. "By minute 10, I've lost 60% of viewers. By the end, maybe 25% are still watching."

When I watched her videos, the problem was obvious: they were structured like lectures. She'd start with the month's data, then spend 12 minutes walking through numbers in sequential order. Prices up 3%, inventory down 8%, days on market increased. On and on. Good information delivered in the most sleep-inducing way possible. Same energy throughout. Same visual of her at a desk with charts. Same pacing. No stories, no surprises, no reason to keep watching once you got the general picture.

We restructured her approach completely. Instead of a sequential data dump, we opened with the most surprising stat teased as a hook:

"One number in this month's data shocked me, and if you're thinking about selling, you need to see this."

Then a quick overview of the top three trends to set expectations. Then three deep-dive segments, each built around a specific trend and illustrated with a real client story showing the impact. B-roll of neighborhoods every 90 seconds. On-screen graphics highlighting key numbers. Camera angle changes between sections. And the "shocking" stat from the hook was held until the 9-minute mark, creating an open loop that pulled viewers through the entire middle section.

The results over 90 days told the story. Average view duration climbed from 38% to 54%. The percentage of viewers still watching at the 10-minute mark jumped from 40% to 62%. Impressions increased 2.4 times because the algorithm rewarded the improved retention. Comments increased because viewers were staying long enough to actually engage. And lead quality improved because prospects who watched longer arrived more educated and ready to act.

Same information. Same expertise. Same topics. The only change was how that information was structured and delivered.

"I used to think structure was just about organization," Jennifer told me. "Now I understand it's about psychology. Every minute of my video needs to earn the next minute."

Does that make sense? Structure isn't just about what you say. It's about the order, pacing, and emotional architecture that keeps a viewer's brain deciding, moment by moment, that staying is worth it.

CRAZY SIMPLE ACTION

Build Your Retention Blueprint

Block 30 minutes before you film your next video. You're building the structural plan that prevents the sagging middle.

- **Pick your structure:** Is it a list video? Use the Countdown. A how-to? Use Problem-Solution. A case study or tour? Use the Story Arc. Step-by-step instruction? Use the Tutorial. Don't try to invent a new format. Pick one of these four and let the proven framework do the heavy lifting. Write down which structure you're using and why it fits.

- **Map your five value peaks:** For each peak, write one sentence describing the specific moment of value. Peak 1 is your hook. Peak 2 hits at the 25% mark with your first major insight. Peak 3 at 50% is your surprise or pivot. Peak 4 at 75% is your most valuable or actionable content. Peak 5 is your close. Then write three tease statements that bridge between peaks: one at 25%, one at 50%, and one at 75%. Each tease should hint at what's coming next without giving it away.

- **Plan your pattern interrupts:** For a 10-minute video, you need at least six. For each one, write down what it is (camera angle change, B-roll, graphic, story break, tone shift) and roughly where it goes. Space them 60 to 90 seconds apart. If you're filming a talking-head video, this planning step is where you decide what B-roll you need to capture and what graphics you need to create.

- **Identify danger zones:** Note your two biggest moments where viewers are most likely to drop off. Usually these are dense information sections, transitions between topics, or the stretch right after your biggest value peak (when viewers feel like they've gotten what they came for). For each danger zone, write your prevention plan: an open loop to tease, a pattern interrupt to deploy, or a value peak to deliver.

Then commit to using this blueprint for every video from this point forward. Structure isn't optional, it's the architecture that keeps viewers watching from first second to last.

In Chapter 11, we'll cover scripting and delivery, how to communicate on camera with confidence, clarity, and authenticity so that your perfectly structured video is also perfectly delivered.

CHAPTER 11
Scripting and Delivery: Finding Your On-Camera Voice

OPENING HOOK

Here's a secret most YouTube gurus won't tell you: you don't need to be naturally charismatic on camera. You don't need to be an entertainer. You don't need that effortless energy some creators seem to have been born with.

What you need is a system.

I've worked with hundreds of business professionals who were convinced they "weren't good on camera." Coaches who froze when the red light came on. Real estate agents who rambled for twenty minutes without making a point. Consultants who sounded like they were reading a legal document. Every single one of them believed their on-camera presence was a fixed trait, something they either had or didn't.

They were wrong. On-camera delivery is a skill, and like any skill, it can be learned, practiced, and systematized.

The breakthrough comes when you realize that great YouTube delivery isn't about performing. It's about communicating clearly with energy. You're not trying to be a TV host. You're trying to be the most engaging version of yourself, explaining something you genuinely know and care about to someone who genuinely wants to learn it.

The key is preparation. Creators who look natural on camera aren't winging it. They've prepared in a way that allows them to be natural. They know exactly what they're going to say, in what order, and with what emphasis. That preparation frees them to focus on delivery rather than content.

This chapter gives you a repeatable process for preparing and delivering videos that sound natural, hold attention, and position you as the expert you are. No acting required.

THE FRAMEWORK

The Scripting Spectrum

There's no single right way to script a video. Different creators work best with different levels of preparation. The key is finding your spot on the spectrum and working from there.

At one end is the full word-for-word script. You write every sentence, every transition, every aside. This works well for complex topics that require precision, for beginners who freeze without structure, and for videos where exact wording matters (think legal or technical content). The challenge is that reading a script often sounds stiff on camera. If you go this route, read the script out loud multiple times before filming. Edit for how the words sound when spoken, not how they read on paper. And consider a teleprompter app so you're not looking down at your notes.

In the middle is the detailed outline, and this is where I recommend most business creators start. You write your main points with key phrases and transitions, but you speak naturally around them. The hook and closing are scripted word-for-word because those are the highest-stakes moments. Everything in between is guided but not rigid. This approach provides structure without killing your personality.

Further down the spectrum is bullet points only. You list topics in order and speak freely about each one. This works if you know your material cold and you're naturally comfortable on camera. The risk is rambling, going off track, or forgetting important points. Even with minimal scripting, always prepare your hook. The first 30 seconds are too important to improvise.

At the far end is full improvisation. No script, no notes. You know your topic and just talk. This is fine for vlogs, reaction content, or Q&A videos. For educational or business content, I don't recommend it. The editing time you'll spend tightening a rambling take almost always exceeds the time you would have spent creating a quick outline.

My recommendation: start with a detailed outline and stay there until you've filmed at least 20 videos. Once you know your rhythm, you can drift toward bullet points. Most successful business YouTubers live somewhere between those two levels permanently.

The Outline Structure

Regardless of how detailed your script is, every video should follow a clear structure. This is the skeleton that keeps your content organized and your viewer engaged.

Your hook takes the first 30 seconds. Script this word-for-word every time. It's too important to wing it. We covered hook techniques in depth in Chapter 9, so you already have the formulas. Your credibility statement follows immediately, taking about 15 to 30 seconds. Not a full bio. Just a sentence or two: "I've helped over 200 clients navigate this exact situation," or "After testing this for six months on my own channel, here's what I found."

Next comes the roadmap, which takes 15 to 30 seconds. Tell viewers what you'll cover: "In this video, I'll show you the three biggest mistakes, then give you the exact framework I use with my clients." This sets expectations and gives viewers a reason to stay because they know the good stuff is coming.

The main content fills the bulk of the video. Structure it in clear sections, each with a point to make, an explanation, an example or story as proof, and a transition to the next section. Think of each section as a mini-video within the larger video. If any section can't justify its existence, cut it.

Your call to action takes 30 to 60 seconds near the end. Don't just stop. Direct viewers to take a specific action: download your lead magnet, watch another video, subscribe, or leave a comment. Be specific about what you want them to do and why it benefits them. Then close in 15 to 30 seconds with a final thought, encouragement, or summary. End strong. The last thing you say is what viewers remember.

Delivery Techniques That Actually Work

Great delivery isn't about being someone you're not. It's about being the most energetic, clear version of yourself. A few techniques make a dramatic difference.

The camera dampens energy. What feels over the top in person reads as normal on screen. Increase your energy by about 20% from your natural speaking style. Speak slightly faster, gesture more, and let your face be more expressive. It will feel weird at first. It looks right on camera. Trust me on this. Almost every person I've coached thinks they're being "too much" when they're actually landing perfectly.

Talk to one person. Don't think of your audience as thousands of viewers. Imagine you're explaining this to one specific person: a friend, a past client, someone who genuinely needs this information. This creates intimacy and prevents the stiff "presenting to a crowd" feeling that kills business content. Some creators put a photo of an actual client next to their camera to maintain that connection.

Vary your pace throughout the video. Monotone delivery kills retention faster than bad lighting. Speed up during exciting or straightforward parts. Slow down for important points you want to land. Pause briefly before key statements to create emphasis. The contrast between fast and slow is what holds attention, the same way a song needs both loud and quiet moments.

Use your hands. Gestures make you appear more confident and help viewers follow your points. Don't keep your hands rigidly at your sides or clasped together. Let them move naturally, as they would in conversation. And look directly at the camera lens, not the screen or viewfinder. Eye contact builds trust. If you struggle with this, put a small sticker, or even a googly eye, right next to the lens as a target.

Finally, embrace imperfection. You don't need perfect takes. Small stumbles, brief pauses to think, even the occasional "um" make you human and relatable. Stop restarting every time you make a minor mistake. Keep rolling and edit later if needed. The pursuit of perfection is what makes most people sound robotic in the first place.

The Five-Minute Pre-Recording Ritual

What you do right before you hit record dramatically impacts your delivery. Build a ritual and use it every time.

Start with a physical warm-up. Shake out your hands and arms. Roll your shoulders. Do a few jumping jacks if you're feeling low energy. Physical movement activates mental energy, and you'd be amazed how much better you sound on camera after 30 seconds of movement versus sitting at your desk and hitting record cold.

Follow with a vocal warm-up. Hum for 30 seconds. Say a few tongue twisters. Read your hook out loud twice. Your voice should be warmed up before the real take, the same way a singer warms up before a performance.

Then do a mental reset. Take three deep breaths. Remind yourself why this content matters and who it will help. Smile before you hit record, even if it feels silly, because it changes your vocal tone even when viewers can't see it. Review your hook one final time so the first sentence rolls off your tongue automatically. Then press record while the energy is high. Don't let it cool down.

Your Script Development Partner

Use this prompt to develop video outlines that sound natural when spoken.

PROMPT: YouTube Video Script Outline

Help me create a detailed outline for a YouTube video.

Video topic: [YOUR TOPIC]

Target length: [X MINUTES]

Target audience: [WHO THIS IS FOR]

Main takeaway: [WHAT VIEWERS SHOULD LEARN/DO]

My speaking style: [CONVERSATIONAL / PROFESSIONAL / ENERGETIC / ETC.]

Please create:

1. A word-for-word hook (first 30 seconds) that creates curiosity

2. A brief credibility statement I can customize

3. A roadmap sentence previewing the content

4. Main content sections with:

o Key point to make

o Talking points (not full script)

o Suggested example or story prompt

o Transition to the next section

5. A call to action that feels natural

6. A strong closing statement

Write for spoken delivery. Use conversational language, short sentences, and natural transitions. Avoid jargon and overly formal phrasing.

This generates a Level 2 outline: detailed enough to guide you, loose enough to sound natural. Read the output aloud and adjust anything that sounds written rather than spoken. Your goal is an outline you can glance at while filming, not a script you read verbatim.

CASE STUDY

From Painful to Natural

Marcus was a financial advisor who had tried YouTube three separate times before working with me. Each time, he'd film a few videos, hate how he looked and sounded, and quit.

"I watched other financial advisors on YouTube who seemed so natural," he said. "I'd try to be like them, but I just sounded fake. Forced. Like I was reading a teleprompter even when I wasn't. After three attempts, I'd convinced myself I just wasn't meant for video."

When I reviewed his old videos, the problems were clear. He was writing full scripts in formal, written language, the kind you'd use in a client report. Then he'd try to memorize them, which made him sound stiff and caused him to freeze whenever he forgot a line. His energy was flat because he was concentrating so hard on remembering words. He never smiled. He barely moved.

We rebuilt his approach in five steps. First, I had him explain his video topic to me in conversation, with no script at all. He was engaging, clear, used great analogies, and had natural energy. I recorded the conversation.

"That's your YouTube voice," I told him. "We just need to capture it."

Second, we moved him from full scripts to detailed outlines. The hook was written word-for-word. Everything else was bullet points, with key phrases noted but no full sentences. This freed him to speak naturally while staying on track.

Third, we built a pre-recording ritual: jumping jacks, vocal warm-ups, three deep breaths, reading the hook twice, and hitting record while the energy was high.

Fourth, we used the "one person" technique. Marcus put a photo of an actual client next to his camera, someone he'd helped successfully, and talked to that photo. His delivery immediately became more conversational and warmer.

Fifth, we broke his addiction to perfect takes. He used to restart every time he stumbled. Now he kept rolling. Most mistakes could be edited out. The ones that couldn't actually made him more relatable.

The transformation was measurable. Filming time per video dropped from 90-plus minutes to 25 minutes. Takes per video went from 15–20 down to two or three. Average viewer retention climbed from 28% to 52%. And viewers started commenting on his delivery specifically: "You make this so easy to understand."

"The irony is I'm more myself now with an outline than I ever was with a full script," Marcus told me later. "The script made me try to be perfect. The outline lets me be human. And human is what connects."

Six months later, Marcus's channel had grown to 8,000 subscribers. More importantly, he actually enjoyed creating videos. What had felt painful now felt natural, because he'd found a system that worked with his personality instead of fighting against it.

CRAZY SIMPLE ACTION

Find Your Scripting Sweet Spot

Block 30 minutes. You're going to build your personal scripting and delivery system so every future video starts from a proven foundation.

- **Assess where you are honestly.** On a scale of 1 to 10, how comfortable are you speaking on camera? What's your biggest delivery challenge: freezing, sounding robotic, rambling, low energy, or needing too many takes? Name the specific problem. If you've never been on camera, your answer is "I don't know yet," and that's fine. Start at a detailed outline (Level 2) and adjust after your first five videos.

- **Build your reusable outline template now.** Write out the skeleton: your hook format (which formula from Chapter 9 you'll default to), your standard credibility statement (one sentence about your experience or results), how you'll structure main content sections, your standard call to action, and your closing. This template stays the same across videos. You customize the content, but the bones stay consistent. Consistency in structure is what makes preparation fast.

- **Design your pre-recording ritual and write it on a card you keep near your camera.** Physical warm-up (what you'll do specifically), vocal warm-up (humming, tongue twisters, reading your hook aloud), mental reset (deep breaths, who you're talking to, why this matters). Do this before every filming session without exception. It takes five minutes and transforms your delivery.

- **Film a practice video this week.** Not for publishing, just for practice. Use your outline template, do your pre-recording ritual, and record yourself talking for five minutes about any topic you know well. Watch it back. Note one thing you'd improve. Then film it again with that adjustment. This single exercise will teach you more about your on-camera presence than reading a hundred books about it. Your delivery will improve with every video you make. The goal isn't perfection. It's progress. Follow your system, trust the process, and know the awkwardness you feel now will fade as the reps accumulate.

In Chapter 12, we'll cover the editing workflow, how to turn your raw footage into polished videos efficiently, without spending hours in post-production.

CHAPTER 12
Editing for Engagement, Not Perfection

OPENING HOOK

I'm going to tell you something that will save you hundreds of hours: your audience doesn't care about your editing.

Not in the way you think they do, anyway.

I've watched creators spend eight hours editing a ten-minute video. Obsessing over color grading. Agonizing over transitions. Adding motion graphics that took longer to create than the filming itself. They publish their masterpiece, convinced that this level of polish is what separates professionals from amateurs.

Then they watch it get outperformed by a competitor's video that was clearly edited in thirty minutes. Jump cuts. Minimal graphics. Maybe a lower third and some basic text on screen. That's it.

The difference? The "poorly" edited video was edited for engagement. The overproduced video was edited for aesthetics. And YouTube's algorithm, along with your viewers, cares about only one of those things.

For business YouTube channels, editing exists for exactly three purposes: removing mistakes that would distract viewers, adding visual elements that improve retention, and making your content easier to consume. That's the entire job description. Everything beyond those three purposes is either procrastination disguised as productivity or ego disguised as professionalism.

I learned this through painful experimentation. Early on, I spent entire weekends on single videos. I learned After Effects just to create custom animated intros. I color-graded footage like I was preparing it for Sundance. My retention actually got worse. Viewers found the production distracting. The fancy editing called attention to itself instead of supporting the content.

When I stripped everything back, when I started editing for engagement instead of admiration, my results transformed. Videos took two hours to edit instead of twelve. I published more frequently. And viewers actually watched longer because nothing was getting in the way of the content they came for.

THE FRAMEWORK

The Engagement Editing Philosophy

Four principles should guide every editing decision you make.

The first is that editing should be invisible. The best editing goes unnoticed. When someone comments, "Great editing!" on a business video, that's actually a warning sign. It means the editing was noticeable enough to pull attention away from the message. Your editing should feel so natural that viewers don't consciously register it at all.

Second, every edit must earn its place. Before adding any element, whether a transition, a graphic, or a sound effect, ask, "Does this help the viewer understand or stay engaged?" If the answer isn't a clear yes, cut it. If a viewer would absorb the information just as well without that element, the element doesn't belong.

Third, speed serves the viewer. Dead air is death. Pauses between sentences, ums and ahs, moments where you're collecting your thoughts, all create opportunities for viewers to click away. Tight editing that removes dead space doesn't feel rushed to viewers. It feels respectful of their time.

Fourth, consistency beats creativity. Developing a consistent editing style, same fonts, same graphics, same pacing, builds brand recognition and makes editing faster. When you're not reinventing your approach every video, you can move through the edit in a fraction of the time.

The Five Edits That Actually Matter

Of all the editing techniques available to you, five actually move the needle for business content. Master these before you consider anything else.

Jump cuts are your most important tool. Cut out pauses, mistakes, and filler words, then place the remaining clips back-to-back. Yes, this creates a visible jump in the video. No, viewers don't care. They barely notice. What they do notice, and hate, is waiting. Cut at the natural end of sentences. Leave just a breath of space between cuts so it doesn't feel frantic. If a jump feels too jarring, cover it with B-roll.

B-roll coverage is secondary footage that plays while your audio continues. For real estate agents, this might be property footage. For coaches, screen recordings or stock footage. B-roll covers distracting jump cuts, provides visual variety that maintains attention, and reinforces your message with supporting imagery. Keep clips short, two to five seconds typically, and make sure the footage supports what you're saying rather than distracting from it. When you don't have custom B-roll, Pexels and Pixabay offer free stock footage that works in a pinch.

On-screen text and graphics reinforce key points and help viewers who are watching without sound (more common than you'd think, especially on mobile). Use lower thirds for your name and title. Display key statistics when you say them. Highlight important terms. Keep it to three or four words maximum on screen at once. Make it large enough to read on a phone. Use consistent fonts and colors across every video. Remove text after three to five seconds. Don't let it linger.

Pattern interrupt cuts break visual monotony every 60 to 90 seconds. A different camera angle. A B-roll sequence. A graphic. Anything that changes what the viewer sees. If you only have one camera angle, B-roll and graphics become even more important. A simple zoom-in on your existing footage, called a "punch in", can create the effect of an angle change without additional filming.

Audio cleanup rounds out the essentials. Bad audio kills videos faster than bad video. Remove background noise using your editing software's built-in noise reduction. Normalize volume so nothing is too quiet or blows out the speakers. Add subtle background music to fill silence and maintain energy, keeping it barely noticeable at -15 to -20 dB while your voice sits at -6 to -12 dB. YouTube's Audio Library has free options. Epidemic Sound and Artlist are paid but worth considering once you're publishing regularly.

The Edits That Waste Your Time

Just as important as knowing what to do is knowing what to skip.

Extensive color grading is the first trap. Unless your footage looks obviously wrong, basic auto-correction is enough. Viewers aren't comparing your color palette to Hollywood films. A simple preset applied consistently is fine. An hour of color grading is not.

Fancy transitions are the second. Swipes. Spins. Dissolves. Star wipes. These scream "amateur trying to look professional." Simple cuts are almost always better. The transition itself should never be memorable.

Motion graphics are the third. Animated logos. Flying text. Elaborate visual effects. They take hours and add almost nothing to engagement. A static graphic that appears for two seconds delivers the same information as an animated one that took three hours to build.

Sound design is the fourth. "Whoosh" sounds on every transition. A "ding" on every text appearance. These feel clever when you're adding them and annoying when you're watching. Minimal sound effects are plenty.

And the fifth, the one that steals more hours than all the others combined, is perfectionism. Watching your edit over and over, finding tiny imperfections to fix. A slightly awkward pause. A graphic that appears one frame too late. A word you stumbled over but recovered from. Viewers watching once will never notice these things. Your perfectionism is serving your ego, not your audience. Export the video and move on.

The Two-Hour Edit Workflow

Here's how to edit a 10- to 15-minute video in approximately two hours, broken into five phases.

Phase one is the rough cut, about 45 minutes. Import your footage and watch it at 1.5x speed while cutting out obvious mistakes, long pauses, and false starts. Don't worry about precision. Just get the content down to approximately the right length. You're sculpting the rough shape.

Phase two is tightening, about 30 minutes. Go through it again, cutting tighter. Remove filler words. Trim pauses between sentences. Cut any tangents that don't serve the main point. The goal is to make every second count.

Phase three is enhancement, about 30 minutes. Add B-roll at planned pattern-interrupt points. Insert text graphics for key points and statistics. Add your lower-third introduction. This is where the video starts looking polished.

Phase four is audio, about 15 minutes. Apply noise reduction if needed. Normalize levels. Add background music at the right volume. Make sure nothing peaks or drops.

Phase five is review and export, about 15 minutes. Watch through once at normal speed. Make only essential fixes, things that would genuinely confuse or distract viewers. Export in 1080p or 4K. Done.

Will this produce cinema-quality content? No. Will it produce content that engages viewers and builds your business? Absolutely. And it will let you publish consistently instead of burning out after three overproduced videos.

Software: What You Actually Need

You don't need expensive software to edit well. For most business creators, CapCut (free) or DaVinci Resolve (the free version is excellent) handles everything in this chapter. Both offer jump cuts, text overlays, B-roll layering, audio cleanup, and background music support. Both run on Mac and PC. Both have YouTube tutorials that can get you proficient in a weekend.

If you're already in the Adobe ecosystem, Premiere Pro works great but costs $23 per month. Descript is worth mentioning because it lets you edit video by editing a text transcript, which means you can cut sections by deleting words rather than scrubbing through a timeline. For business creators who find traditional editing interfaces intimidating, Descript can cut your learning curve in half.

Whatever software you pick, commit to it for at least six months before switching. The biggest time waste in editing isn't the editing itself. It's constantly learning new tools because someone on YouTube convinced you that a different app would be faster. The best editing software is the one you know well enough to move through without thinking about it. Speed comes from familiarity, not features.

AI INTEGRATION

Your Editing Decision Assistant

Use this prompt when you're tempted to add an editing element and need a reality check on whether it's worth your time.

PROMPT: YouTube Editing ROI Evaluator

Help me decide if this editing element is worth my time.

Editing element I'm considering: [DESCRIBE IT]

Estimated time to implement: [X MINUTES/HOURS]

My content type: [Educational/Tutorial/Tour/etc.]

My current publishing frequency: [HOW OFTEN]

Please evaluate:

1. Will this measurably improve viewer retention?

2. Will viewers notice if this element is missing?

3. Is this time better spent on content or promotion?

4. Is this serving my audience or my ego?

5. What's the minimum viable version that achieves 80% of the benefit?

Give me a clear recommendation: implement as planned, implement the minimum version, or skip.

This is especially useful when you discover a new editing technique and think, "I should do that." Just because something looks impressive doesn't mean it's worth your hours. The question is always: does this serve the viewer's experience, or just your desire to look professional?

CASE STUDY

The Editor Who Learned to Let Go

Marcus, the financial advisor we met in Chapter 11, had a second problem we hadn't addressed yet: his production background was killing his publishing frequency.

Before getting into financial advising, Marcus had worked as a videographer for a local TV station. He knew After Effects. He could color-grade like a professional colorist. He understood three-point lighting and audio mixing. When he started his YouTube channel, he approached every video like a broadcast production.

Each video took 12 to 15 hours to edit. Custom animated graphics. Every cut smoothed with a transition. Perfect color grading. Professionally mixed audio. The result was beautiful content that nobody saw because he was publishing once a month. Sometimes less.

Meanwhile, a competitor in his market was publishing three times per week with basic talking-head footage, jump cuts, and simple text on screen. Nothing fancy. But the competitor's channel was growing because the videos were helpful, consistent, and everywhere.

"He was beating me with videos I considered amateur," Marcus admitted. "That's when I realized I had the equation completely wrong."

We stripped his editing process down to the essentials from this chapter. No more custom animations. No transitions except simple cuts. Color correction limited to one preset applied to all footage. Audio cleanup capped at 10 minutes. Total editing time per video capped at two hours.

"The first few videos were painful," he said. "I kept seeing things I wanted to fix, effects I wanted to add. I had to physically stop myself from going back into the edit."

But his metrics didn't suffer. Average view duration stayed the same. Click-through rate stayed the same. Comments actually increased. People were engaging with his content just as much as before.

Over six months, his publishing frequency jumped from once a month to twice a week. Total videos published increased eightfold. Subscribers grew from 400 to 4,200. Monthly YouTube leads went from two or three to 15 to 20. And the total time he spent editing per month actually dropped from 15-plus hours to eight hours, even though he was creating eight times more content.

"The production quality I was so proud of wasn't what viewers valued," Marcus reflected. "They valued the information. They valued consistency. They valued feeling like they knew me because I showed up regularly. None of that required fancy editing."

CRAZY SIMPLE ACTION

Build Your Editing Template

Block 45 minutes. You're building the reusable editing system that makes every future video faster.

- **Spend 10 minutes auditing your current process.** How long does editing actually take per video? Where does the time go? Be honest about whether you're spending hours on elements that viewers would never miss. If you haven't started editing yet, skip to the next step and build your system before bad habits form.

- **Spend 15 minutes defining your essentials and building a template in your editing software.** Your template should include your intro style (if any), your lower-third graphic, your text style for key points (font, color, size, placement), your background music approach, and your outro. Create these once. Save them as a project template. Every future video starts from this template, which means you never rebuild these elements from scratch.

- **Spend 5 minutes setting your time budget.** Decide on a maximum editing time per video and write it down. For most business channels, two hours is the right cap. Allocate that time across the five phases: rough cut, tightening, enhancement, audio, and review. When your timer hits the cap, you export and publish. No exceptions.

- **Make the commitment out loud and in writing.** Post this near wherever you edit: "A good video published beats a perfect video in progress. My job is to serve my audience with consistent, helpful content, not to win editing awards." Your next video will be edited using your template, within your time budget. The discomfort you feel when letting go of perfectionism is the feeling of choosing effectiveness over ego. Embrace it.

In Chapter 13, we'll cover publishing and optimization, how to set your video up for maximum discoverability from the moment it goes live.

CHAPTER 13
Publishing and Optimization: The Launch Sequence

OPENING HOOK

You've done everything right. A great topic people are searching for. A compelling title and thumbnail. A strong hook. Solid structure. A clean edit. Your video is genuinely good.

Then you click publish, and nothing happens.

A hundred views in the first week. Maybe two hundred. Your video disappears into the void, never to be seen by the audience who would have loved it.

This happens constantly, and it's heartbreaking to watch. Creators pour hours into making great content, then throw it away with a careless publishing process. They upload without optimizing their metadata. They ignore the critical first 48 hours. They never touch the video again after it goes live.

Publishing isn't the end of the process. It's the beginning of a launch. What you do in the moments before, during, and after publishing can mean the difference between a video that reaches thousands and one that reaches dozens.

YouTube is constantly testing your content. When a new video goes live, the algorithm shows it to a small sample of viewers and watches carefully. Do they click? Do they watch? Do they engage? Based on those early signals, YouTube decides whether to push your video to more people or let it fade away.

I've seen creators double their average views simply by optimizing their publishing process. Same content quality. Same topics. Same thumbnails. The only difference was treating publishing as a strategic event rather than an afterthought.

On my own channels, I developed a publishing checklist that I use for every single video. It takes maybe fifteen minutes of extra work per upload, but the compounding effect across hundreds of videos has generated millions of additional views. That's not an exaggeration. It's the mathematical reality of optimizing a repeatable process across a growing library.

THE FRAMEWORK

The Pre-Publish Checklist

Before you click that publish button, every element of your video's metadata should be locked and loaded. Rushing this step is one of the most common and costly mistakes creators make.

Give your title one final review. Does it include your target keyword near the beginning? Does it create curiosity or promise clear value? Is it under 60 characters so it doesn't get cut off in search results? Would you click on it if you saw it in your feed? This final check catches issues you missed when you wrote the title days or weeks ago.

Your video description is prime real estate that most creators waste. The first 150 characters appear in search results without clicking "Show more," so treat those characters like a second headline: include your main keyword and a compelling reason to watch. The first full paragraph should expand on what the video covers, naturally weaving in your primary keyword and any secondary search terms. Write for humans first, but know that YouTube reads this for ranking.

If your video has clear sections, add timestamps formatted as "0:00" with a label, and YouTube will automatically create chapters. These improve the viewer experience and can help you appear in search results for specific subtopics. After your timestamps, place your links: lead magnet first (it gets the most clicks), then booking or consultation links, then your website. Close with a brief, consistent bio section that you copy and paste into every video.

Tags matter less than they used to, but they're still worth doing correctly. YouTube uses them to understand your content and find related videos. Lead with your exact target keyword as the first tag, followed by two or three variations, two or three broader category tags, and your channel name. Keep total tags under 500 characters.

Don't stuff irrelevant tags hoping to game the system. YouTube catches that now, and it can actually hurt your discoverability.

Upload your custom thumbnail rather than using a video frame. Double-check that it looks sharp at small sizes by viewing the upload preview on your phone. Add the video to relevant playlists before publishing, which helps YouTube understand your content's context and increases the chance of being suggested after related content. Configure your end screen with a subscribe button and at least one video suggestion. Add cards sparingly at relevant points to direct viewers to related content without being distracting.

This entire pre-publish process should take 10 to 15 minutes once you have your templates in place. The first time you build your description template will take longer. Every time after that is copy, paste, customize. That 15-minute investment compounds across every video you ever publish.

The Timing Decision

When you publish matters, but probably not in the way you think.

The conventional wisdom is to publish when your audience is most active, which YouTube Studio shows you. The logic seems sound: publish when they're watching, and more people will see it immediately. But here's the nuance: immediate views matter less than early engagement rate. YouTube isn't measuring how many views you get in the first hour. It's measuring what percentage of people who see your video actually click, and what percentage of those who click keep watching.

For smaller channels under 10,000 subscribers, the timing of your publish matters relatively little. Your video isn't going viral in the first hour regardless. What matters more is consistency. Pick a day and time, stick to it, and let your audience learn when to expect new content. If you're targeting a local audience, publish in your local morning to give the video all-day exposure. Avoid publishing late at night when engagement will be slow. But don't overthink this. Consistency beats optimization every time.

YouTube's scheduling feature is invaluable here. Upload videos and schedule them to publish later so you maintain consistency even when your week gets busy. Batch film and edit on your dedicated production day, then schedule your content to go live at your regular time. This is how you maintain a weekly cadence even during your busiest stretches.

The First 48 Hours

The 48 hours after publishing are your video's most critical period. YouTube is actively evaluating whether to push your content to a wider audience. Here's how to maximize this window.

In the first hour, pin a comment with a question or call to action to encourage engagement. Share the video across your social platforms with a compelling hook customized for each platform. Post in relevant communities, groups, or forums without being spammy. Email your list if you have one. Watch for early comments so you can respond immediately. Every reply you leave counts as engagement and notifies the original commenter, often bringing them back to continue the conversation.

During the first 24 hours, respond to every single comment. Not with generic "Thanks!" replies, but with substantive responses that encourage further discussion. Ask follow-up questions to keep conversations going. Heart comments to acknowledge viewers even when a full reply isn't needed. This active engagement signals to YouTube that your content is generating genuine interest. Here's why this matters so much: every reply you leave counts as additional engagement and sends a notification to the original commenter, which often brings them back to continue the conversation or watch more of your content. That creates a virtuous cycle that the algorithm rewards.

At the 48-hour mark, check your analytics. How does your CTR compare to your channel average? Review the retention graph for unusual drop-off points. If CTR is below your average after 48 hours, consider testing a different thumbnail. YouTube's algorithm gives videos a fresh chance when thumbnails change significantly. Note what worked and what didn't for future reference.

Post-Publish Optimization

Your video isn't frozen in time after it goes live. Strategic updates can revive underperforming content or accelerate videos that are gaining traction.

Thumbnail testing is the most powerful post-publish lever. If your CTR is lagging after 48 hours, swap in a new thumbnail. Create two or three variations before publishing so you can switch quickly without scrambling. Give each version at least 48 to 72 hours of data before judging results. Titles can also be updated without penalty. If search traffic is lower than expected, adjust the title to better match what people are actually searching for. Just be careful not to change it so dramatically that it no longer reflects your content.

Description updates are equally painless. Add timestamps if you didn't include them initially. Update links if your offers change. Add relevant keywords if you discover search terms you missed. Your description can be edited anytime without affecting the video's standing with the algorithm. Think of your published videos as living documents, not fixed products.

Here's something that surprises many creators: YouTube videos often don't peak in their first week. Unlike social media posts with a short shelf life, YouTube videos can grow for months or years. A video might get 500 views in its first month, then suddenly take off six months later as the algorithm finds a new audience for it. This means your evergreen content should be treated as a long-term asset. Revisit old videos periodically. Update thumbnails on your best performers. Refresh descriptions with current links. Your back catalog can become a growing source of views and leads long after you've moved on to new topics.

AI INTEGRATION

Your Publishing Optimization Assistant

Use this prompt to generate optimized metadata for any video before publishing.

PROMPT: YouTube Video Metadata Optimizer

Help me create optimized metadata for my YouTube video.

Video title: [YOUR WORKING TITLE]

Main topic/keyword: [PRIMARY SEARCH TERM]

Video summary: [2–3 SENTENCES ABOUT THE VIDEO]

Key timestamps: [MAJOR SECTIONS WITH APPROX TIMES]

My lead magnet/offer: [WHAT I WANT VIEWERS TO DO]

My website: [URL]

Target audience: [WHO THIS VIDEO IS FOR]

Please generate:

1. An optimized video description with:

o   A compelling first 150 characters with the keyword
o   A full first paragraph (3–4 sentences)
o   Formatted timestamps
o   A CTA section with the lead magnet
o   A standard about/subscribe section

2. A list of 8–10 relevant tags

3. Three hashtags for the description

4. A pinned comment to drive engagement

5. A short social media caption for promotion

Make all copy sound natural, not keyword-stuffed.

Run this before publishing every video. Having your metadata ready in advance means you can upload, paste everything in, and launch without scrambling to write descriptions on the fly. Save your outputs so you can reference what's worked well and maintain consistency.

CASE STUDY

The Launch Sequence That Changed Everything

Rachel was a business coach posting videos consistently, but her results were frustratingly inconsistent. Some videos would get 2,000 views; others with seemingly similar content would stall at 300. She couldn't figure out the pattern.

"I thought it was random," she told me. "I figured some topics just resonated more than others, and there was nothing I could do about it."

When I audited her channel, the problem jumped off the screen: her publishing process was chaos. Sometimes she'd write detailed descriptions; sometimes she'd leave them nearly blank. Sometimes she'd promote new videos on social media; sometimes she'd forget. She had no consistent thumbnail style. Her videos weren't organized into playlists. She rarely responded to comments in the first 24 hours because she was "too busy." She was leaving every video's success entirely to chance.

We built her a simple publishing checklist, a document she would work through before and after every upload. Before hitting publish: title reviewed for keyword and length; description following a consistent template with hook, summary, timestamps, links, and bio; tags added with the primary keyword first; custom thumbnail uploaded and checked at mobile size; video added to a playlist; end screen and cards configured.

After publishing: pin an engaging comment within five minutes. Share to Instagram, LinkedIn, and Facebook with custom captions for each platform. Send an email notification to her list. Set phone reminders to check and respond to comments at hours 3, 6, and 24. At the 48-hour mark, review CTR and retention and decide whether a thumbnail swap is needed.

The total time this added to her process? About 20 to 25 minutes per video.

Over 90 days, the results were dramatic. Average views per video climbed from 650 to 1,800. The consistency of her results improved even more than the averages because the wild swings between hits and misses disappeared. Every video performed at least reasonably well because every video received a proper launch. Average comments per video jumped from 4 to 18. Her subscriber growth rate increased 2.3x. Lead magnet downloads from YouTube went from 8 per month to 34.

"The biggest shift was mental," Rachel said. "I stopped thinking of publishing as the finish line and started thinking of it as the starting gun.

I used to dread checking my analytics. Now I actually look forward to it because I know I've done everything I can to give each video a fair shot."

CRAZY SIMPLE ACTION

Build Your Launch Checklist

Block 20 minutes. You're building the publishing checklist that every future video will use.

- Create a pre-publish checklist in a document or note you'll reference every time you upload. It should include your title review (keyword, length, clarity), description template (150-character hook, summary paragraph, timestamps, links section, bio), tag strategy, thumbnail upload and mobile-size check, playlist assignment, and end screen configuration. Write it once. Reuse it forever. The point isn't to remember this list. The point is to never have to remember it because it's written down.

- Create a post-publish checklist covering the first 48 hours. Include your pinned comment (write a default template you can customize per video), the specific platforms where you'll share (list them by name so there's no ambiguity), your comment response schedule (specific times you'll check), and your 48-hour analytics review with decision criteria for thumbnail swaps. The more specific this checklist is, the less willpower each launch requires.

- Build your description template right now. Write out the complete format with placeholder text: your standard opening line structure, where timestamps go, your standard CTA paragraph with lead magnet language, and your bio/subscribe section. Save this as a template you can copy and paste into every video and customize in two minutes. Most of your description should be identical across videos. Only the topic-specific content changes.

- Commit to the system. No video gets published without completing both checklists. No exceptions. No shortcuts. No "I'll do the description later." Every video deserves a proper launch. The discipline of consistent execution is what separates channels that grow predictably from channels that simply hope for the best. Print your checklists. Tape them next to your desk. Use them starting with your very next upload.

In Chapter 14, we'll build your content calendar and sustainable publishing schedule, because consistency beats intensity every time.

CHAPTER 14
Building Your Content Calendar: Consistency That Lasts

OPENING HOOK

I'm going to tell you about the creator who posts three videos one week, disappears for a month, then comes back with a burst of guilt-fueled uploads before vanishing again.

You probably know this creator. You might be this creator.

The feast-or-famine approach to YouTube feels productive in the moment. When inspiration strikes, you ride the wave, filming multiple videos, editing late into the night, publishing in rapid succession. You feel unstoppable. Then life happens. Work gets busy. The kids need attention. You're tired. The camera sits untouched. Days turn into weeks. Weeks turn into months.

When you finally return, your momentum is gone. Your audience has forgotten you. YouTube's algorithm has deprioritized your channel. You're essentially starting over. Again.

This pattern destroys more YouTube channels than bad content ever will. It's not that these creators lack talent, knowledge, or even time. They lack a sustainable system.

YouTube rewards consistency more than quality. I know that stings. We all want to believe our brilliant one-off video will change everything. But YouTube's algorithm is designed to promote creators who show up reliably, because those are the creators who keep viewers coming back to the platform.

I learned this the hard way with @VanLife. My biggest growth periods didn't coincide with my best content. They coincided with my most consistent publishing. When I showed up every single week without fail, the algorithm noticed. Views climbed. Subscribers grew. Leads came in. And when I fell off schedule, even for two or three weeks, I could watch the metrics slide backward in real time. The same pattern played out with @GotCoach. Once I locked in a consistent schedule, the channel grew faster than it ever had during my "post when inspired" phase. Consistency isn't glamorous. But it's the single highest-ROI behavior on YouTube.

So this chapter isn't about motivation, discipline, or willpower. Those are unreliable fuel sources. This chapter is about building a system that makes consistency the default, not the exception.

THE FRAMEWORK

The Publishing Frequency Sweet Spot

Before you build a calendar, you need to pick a frequency you can actually maintain. Not the frequency you want to maintain when you're feeling ambitious on a Sunday night. The frequency you can sustain during your busiest season, when clients are calling, showings are stacked, and you'd rather collapse on the couch than set up a camera.

Once per week is the minimum for meaningful growth. That gives you 52 videos in a year, enough to build real momentum. YouTube's algorithm takes notice when you publish weekly, and your audience starts to expect and anticipate your content.

Twice per week is the sweet spot for accelerated growth. The data backs this up across nearly every niche I've studied. Two videos per week roughly doubles your growth rate compared to one. You get more data, more opportunities for the algorithm to recommend you, and more reasons for viewers to subscribe.

Three times per week hits diminishing returns unless you're full-time or have a team. For most business owners, especially real estate agents juggling transactions, this pace leads straight back to the feast-or-famine cycle. And less than weekly means painfully slow growth. The algorithm deprioritizes channels that don't publish consistently. If you truly can't commit to weekly, you're better off posting every other week reliably than posting three weeks in a row and then going silent for two months.

Here's the critical rule: choose the frequency you can maintain during your busiest season. If you're a real estate agent and spring is chaos, build your calendar around what spring allows. If you can only do one video per week during your peak season, then one video per week is your schedule. Period. You can always add more during slower months, but your baseline has to survive your busiest months.

The Content Batching System

The single biggest reason creators fall off their schedule isn't a lack of time. It's the energy cost of context switching. When you try to plan, film, edit, and publish one video at a time, every single video requires you to mentally restart the entire process. That's exhausting. And it's completely unnecessary.

Batching means grouping similar tasks together. It eliminates context switching while significantly cutting your total production time. Here's how the monthly batch method works.

Set aside a planning day in week one, about two to three hours. Pick all your topics for the month. Do your keyword research. Write your titles. Create rough outlines for each video. This is a thinking day with no camera and no editing software. Just you, your notes, and the topics that will serve your audience for the next four weeks.

Then schedule a filming day in week one or two, about four to six hours. Set up your equipment once and film all four to eight videos in a single session. Wear the same outfit if you want the flexibility to publish in any order. Start with the topic you're most excited about to build momentum, then power through the rest. You'll be surprised how much faster videos two through six go once you're warmed up.

The same-outfit hack deserves special mention. When I film four videos in a row wearing the same shirt, viewers can't tell they were filmed on the same day. But it gives me complete flexibility to publish them in any order based on what's happening in the market. If rates drop unexpectedly and I have a video about rate changes ready, I can move it to the front of the queue without it looking out of sequence.

Spread your editing across weeks two through four. Edit one or two videos per week, schedule them in YouTube Studio, and let them publish automatically. You're never scrambling to create content because it's already filmed and waiting.

I want to be specific about what batching does to your time. When you create one video at a time from scratch, the total process, including planning, setup, filming, editing, and publishing, typically takes four to five hours. Multiply that by four weeks, and you're at 16 to 20 hours per month. With monthly batching, the same four videos take roughly 10 to 12 hours total because you eliminate repetitive setup, warm-up, and context-switching costs. That's 6 to 8 hours saved every month. Over a year, that's 72 to 96 hours, almost two full workweeks returned to you.

The math on batching is ridiculous. And I've never met a creator who tried it and went back to the one-at-a-time approach.

The Content Mix Strategy

Not every video should serve the same purpose. The most successful channels I've coached run a deliberate content mix, and the ratio I've seen work best breaks down into three categories.

Pillar content should make up about 50 to 60% of your videos. These are your evergreen, search-focused workhorses. They answer the questions people are typing into YouTube right now, and will still be typing a year from now. "How to buy your first home in [city]" or "5 things to know before selling your house." These bring in steady traffic month after month and form the backbone of your searchable library.

Trending or timely content should account for 20 to 30%. These respond to what's happening right now: market shifts, interest rate changes, seasonal buying patterns, new developments in your area. They spike in views quickly and show the algorithm that your channel is active and relevant. They also demonstrate to your audience that you're plugged in and paying attention.

Connection content fills the remaining 10 to 20%. Behind-the-scenes tours, Q&A sessions, day-in-the-life content, personal stories about your journey. These build the human relationship that turns viewers into actual clients. People don't hire a YouTube algorithm. They hire a person they feel they know and trust.

Plot this mix across your monthly calendar and you'll never run out of ideas. Week one might be a pillar video and a trending update. Week two could be a pillar video and a connection piece. The variety keeps your audience engaged, while the pillar content drives consistent search traffic.

Surviving the Inevitable Break

Life is going to get in the way. Over the course of a year, you will have weeks when publishing feels impossible. The difference between creators who survive these weeks and those who spiral into months-long absences comes down to preparation.

First, always work at least two weeks ahead of your publish date. When you batch film and edit in advance, you've built a buffer. If a crazy week hits, you've got content already scheduled and ready to go. You don't have to create anything. You just let the system run.

Second, build an emergency stash. Film two or three evergreen videos that aren't time-sensitive and keep them in your back pocket. If your buffer runs dry, pull one of these out. "7 mistakes first-time homebuyers make" works whether you publish it in March or September.

Third, have a reduced-frequency plan ready before you need it. If you normally publish twice a week and life gets hectic, drop to once a week temporarily. That's infinitely better than dropping to zero. The algorithm can handle a frequency reduction. What it can't handle is a complete disappearance.

And if you do need to take a significant break, tell your audience. A quick community post or final video saying, "I'm taking two weeks off, back on this date," maintains trust and gives viewers something to look forward to. Unexplained disappearances erode subscriber loyalty. Explained breaks don't.

AI INTEGRATION

Your Content Calendar Builder

Use this prompt at the start of each quarter to generate a customized content calendar. Having 12 weeks planned in advance eliminates the daily "What should I create?" decision paralysis.

PROMPT: YouTube Content Calendar Generator

Help me create a content calendar for my YouTube

channel.

My niche: [YOUR INDUSTRY/TOPIC]

Target audience: [WHO YOU SERVE]

Publishing frequency: [HOW OFTEN YOU CAN COMMIT]

Busiest time of year: [WHEN YOU HAVE LEAST TIME]

Seasonal trends: [ANY RELEVANT TIMING]

My 5 core topics: [LIST MAIN CONTENT PILLARS]

Please create:

1. A 12-week content calendar with specific topics

2. Label each video as Pillar, Trending, or Connection content

3. Include a working title for each video

4. Note which videos could be batched together

5. Identify 3 evergreen topics for my emergency stash

6. Suggest how to adjust during my busy season

Target mix: 60% pillar, 25% trending, 15% connection content.

Keep your generated calendars in a document and review them quarterly. You'll start to notice patterns: which topics performed well, which felt forced, and what's missing. This historical data makes future planning even more effective.

CASE STUDY

From Chaos to Calendar

Mike was the classic feast-or-famine creator. A real estate agent in Colorado, he'd get excited about YouTube, post four videos in two weeks, then disappear for six weeks. Then guilt would kick in, he'd post a few more, and the cycle would repeat.

"I always had good intentions," he told me. "But then a hot listing would come in, or I'd have a family commitment, and YouTube would fall off. I'd tell myself I'd get back to it, but weeks would pass."

In eighteen months of this pattern, he'd published 31 videos, an average of less than two per month. His subscriber count had barely moved. Views were inconsistent. He was ready to quit.

We rebuilt his approach from the ground up. Not with more motivation or accountability tricks, but with a system.

First, we set a realistic frequency: one video per week. Not two, even though he wanted to. One. We chose Monday for publishing because his slowest day for real estate was Sunday, which gave him a natural filming and editing window.

Second, we implemented monthly batch filming. The first Sunday of every month, he films four videos. Same location, same outfit, four different topics. Total filming time: about three hours.

Third, we built his safety net. A two-week buffer of scheduled content, three evergreen emergency stash videos, and a reduced-frequency plan for his busy spring season, when he knew he'd be buried in transactions.

Over the next twelve months, the results told the story. He published 52 videos. Zero missed weeks. Subscribers went from 340 to 4,100. Leads went from 2 to 3 per year to 4 to 5 per month. He used his emergency stash twice and his reduced-frequency plan once during spring.

"The system freed me," Mike said. "I stopped thinking about YouTube as this thing I had to constantly decide to do. It was just built into my month. Like paying my bills or going to the gym. It wasn't a question anymore."

Mike's content quality didn't change dramatically. His equipment was the same. His on-camera presence was the same. What changed was that he showed up every single week, and YouTube rewarded that consistency with exponential growth.

CRAZY SIMPLE ACTION

Build Your Sustainable System

Block 30 minutes. You're building the content system that makes consistency automatic.

- Do the reality check first. How many hours per week can you realistically dedicate to YouTube during your busiest season? What day is most open for filming? What day works best for editing? Be honest with yourself, because the answers to these questions determine everything that follows. Based on your honest assessment, choose your publishing frequency: once a week if you have two to three hours available, twice a week if you have four to six. Write it down. This is your commitment.

- Design your monthly batch schedule. Pick your planning day, your filming day, and your editing rhythm. Block these on your actual calendar as recurring appointments right now. Treat them like client meetings that cannot be moved. The batch schedule is what transforms YouTube from an ongoing burden into a predictable monthly routine.

- Build your safety net before you need it. Write down three evergreen video topics that would work any time of year for your emergency stash. Decide on your reduced-frequency plan: what's the minimum you can publish when life gets chaotic? When is your busiest season, and how will you handle it? Having these answers ready now means you'll never panic when disruptions hit.

- Plan your first four weeks of content right now. Write down the specific video topic for each week, label it as pillar, trending, or connection content, and note which videos you'll batch film together. Then make the commitment: this calendar is now non-negotiable. The viewers you'll reach, the leads you'll generate, and the business you'll build all depend on showing up consistently. Not perfectly. Consistently.

In Chapter 15, we'll dive into analytics, how to read your numbers, which metrics actually matter, and how to turn data into decisions that accelerate your growth.

CHAPTER 15
Analytics That Actually Matter: Reading Your Data

OPENING HOOK

YouTube Studio gives you access to hundreds of data points. Views, watch time, impressions, click-through rate, average view duration, traffic sources, demographics, real-time analytics, revenue reports, subscriber graphs.

It's overwhelming. And most creators respond in one of two ways.

The first group ignores analytics entirely. They create content based on gut instinct, never checking whether their assumptions are correct. They might spend months making videos in a style that doesn't work, completely unaware that the data is screaming at them to change course.

The second group drowns in data. They check analytics multiple times per day, obsessing over every fluctuation. They see a video underperform and spiral into doubt. They see a video overperform and try to reverse-engineer lightning in a bottle. They're so focused on numbers that they forget to actually create content.

Both approaches are wrong. Analytics should be neither ignored nor obsessed over. They should be used strategically, periodically, and with a clear understanding of what the numbers actually mean.

Here's what I've learned after years of studying analytics across multiple channels: most of the metrics YouTube shows you don't matter. They're interesting. They're fun to look at. But they don't drive decisions that improve your channel. The metrics that actually matter are a small subset of what's available.

When I started treating analytics as a diagnostic tool rather than a scorecard, everything changed. I stopped checking daily and started reviewing weekly. I stopped reacting to individual videos and started identifying patterns across my content. I stopped celebrating vanity metrics and started focusing on the numbers that predicted real business results.

The result was clarity. I knew exactly why some videos succeeded and others didn't. I could predict which content would perform before I published it. I made decisions based on evidence rather than emotion. This chapter gives you that same clarity by showing you which metrics drive growth, how to read YouTube Studio like a dashboard, and how to build a 15-minute weekly routine that gives you everything you need.

THE FRAMEWORK

The Five Metrics That Drive Growth

Click-through rate (CTR) measures the percentage of people who click your video after seeing the thumbnail and title. It tells you whether your packaging is compelling enough to earn attention. A 2–4% CTR is typical, 4–6% is good, and above 6% is excellent. Context matters: CTR naturally decreases as videos are pushed to broader audiences, so a slightly lower CTR on a viral video isn't necessarily bad. If your CTR is consistently below your channel average, that's a thumbnail and title problem. Revisit those skills.

Average view duration (AVD) is YouTube's primary signal for content quality. It measures how long viewers watch before leaving. High AVD tells the algorithm your content delivers value. The target is 50% or higher for most content. Under 40% suggests structural problems: either your hook isn't working, your content doesn't match expectations, or you're losing viewers in the middle. When AVD is low, your retention graph (which I'll cover next) tells you exactly where to look.

Average percentage viewed is related to AVD but gives you a percentage that's easier to compare across videos of different lengths. A 15-minute video with 50% viewed is performing better than a 5-minute video with 40% viewed, even if the raw watch time is similar. The same targets apply as AVD: aim for 50% or higher, and use this metric to compare across your library and identify which types of content hold attention best.

Impressions indicate how much YouTube is promoting your content. Growing impressions over time mean the algorithm is showing your videos to more people. Declining impressions mean it's pulling back. There's no universal benchmark because this depends entirely on your channel size and niche. What matters is the trend: are impressions growing month over month? You can't directly control impressions, but improving CTR and AVD causes YouTube to reward you with more of them.

Subscriber conversion rate measures how many new subscribers you gain per 1,000 views. One to two per thousand is typical; three to five is strong. For business channels targeting a niche audience, rates can run higher because viewers are more qualified. If conversion is low, evaluate whether your content clearly communicates the ongoing value of subscribing. Viewers need a reason to believe future videos will be worth their time.

Reading the Retention Graph

The retention graph is the most actionable piece of data YouTube provides. Find it in YouTube Studio under Content, select a video, then Analytics, then Engagement, then Audience Retention. It shows you exactly where viewers leave your video, which tells you exactly what needs to improve.

Almost every video shows a steep drop in the first 30 seconds. That's normal. Some viewers click and immediately realize the video isn't for them. What matters is the severity. If you're losing 50% in the first 30 seconds, your hook needs serious work. If you're only losing 20–30%, you're doing well.

After the initial drop, watch for sudden cliffs at specific timestamps. These sharp drops indicate something went wrong at that exact moment: a boring section, a confusing explanation, a broken promise. Identify the timestamp, rewatch that section, and figure out what caused viewers to bail. Then make sure you don't repeat it.

A slow, steady decline throughout the video is normal. Viewers naturally leave over time. What you want to avoid is an accelerating decline, where the line gets steeper as the video progresses, because that means your content is becoming less engaging, not more. Conversely, sections where retention stays flat or even bumps up indicate strong content. Viewers aren't leaving, and they might even be rewatching. Identify what made those sections compelling and do more of it.

Most videos show a sharp drop in the final 10–20% as viewers sense the video wrapping up. That's expected. But if the drop starts much earlier, at the 70% mark, for instance, your video might be too long or your ending might be dragging.

Here's the retention-graph hack most creators miss: compare retention graphs across multiple videos to find your personal pattern. Most creators have a consistent weakness. Maybe you always lose people around the two-minute mark because your transitions between sections are weak. Maybe you consistently hold viewers through the middle but lose them at the end because your closings drag. Once you identify your recurring pattern, you can address it systematically rather than treating each video as an isolated problem.

The Metrics That Mislead

Some metrics look important but often lead creators astray.

Total views and total watch time feel significant, but they tell you nothing about quality. A video with 10,000 views and 30% retention is actually worse for your channel than one with 5,000 views and 60% retention, because YouTube evaluates engagement rate, not raw volume.

Likes and comments provide nice social proof, but they don't strongly correlate with growth. Many successful videos have minimal engagement. Some heavily commented videos fail to grow the channel at all. Don't optimize for comments at the expense of retention.

The real-time view counter is pure anxiety fuel. Checking it multiple times per day teaches you nothing and only increases stress. Resist the temptation.

And revenue, at least initially, is a distraction. Until your channel is generating significant views, AdSense earnings are pocket change. Focus on growth. Revenue follows at scale.

I see creators get paralyzed by these vanity metrics all the time. They'll come to me devastated because a video "only" got 500 views, when the real story is that those 500 viewers watched 65% of the video and 12 of them became leads. That's a win by any business metric. But the creator couldn't see it because they were fixated on the wrong number.

Train yourself to ask, "Did this video do its job?" instead of, "Did this video go viral?"

The Weekly 15-Minute Routine

You don't need to live in YouTube Studio. You just need 15 minutes, once per week, following a consistent routine.

Start with a **channel overview**, about three minutes. Open YouTube Studio's Analytics and look at the last 28 days compared to the previous 28 days. Are views, watch time, and subscribers trending up or down? Don't panic over small fluctuations. You're looking for meaningful trends.

Next, **review recent video performance**, about five minutes. For each video published in the last two weeks, check CTR, AVD, and impressions. How do these compare to your channel averages? Flag anything significantly below average for investigation.

Then do a **retention deep-dive** on your most recent video, about five minutes. Examine the retention graph. Where did viewers drop off? Watch those sections. What could you improve? Make a concrete note for your next video.

Close with **pattern recognition**, about two minutes. Step back and look across your recent videos. Are certain topics outperforming others? Are longer or shorter videos working better? Are thumbnails with certain styles getting higher CTR? Document any insights.

That's it. Fifteen minutes once per week gives you everything you need to continuously improve without drowning in analysis.

AI INTEGRATION

Your Analytics Interpreter

Use this prompt during your monthly deep-dive to identify patterns you might be missing in your weekly reviews.

PROMPT: YouTube Analytics Diagnosis

Help me understand my YouTube analytics and what to do about them.

- My channel niche: [YOUR TOPIC/INDUSTRY]

- Current subscriber count: [NUMBER]

- Average views per video: [NUMBER]

For my recent videos (last 5–10):

- Average CTR: [X%]

- Average View Duration: [X minutes or X%]

- Subscriber conversion: [X per 1,000 views]

Best performing video: [TITLE]

- CTR: [X%], AVD: [X%], Views: [NUMBER]

Worst performing video: [TITLE]

- CTR: [X%], AVD: [X%], Views: [NUMBER]

My specific concern: [WHAT'S WORRYING YOU]

Please provide:

1. Diagnosis of what these numbers reveal

2. The one metric I should prioritize improving

3. Three specific actions based on this data

4. How my numbers compare to niche benchmarks

5. What I should NOT worry about right now

The weekly routine keeps you informed. The monthly AI-assisted analysis keeps you strategic. Together, they ensure you're always improving based on evidence rather than guessing.

CASE STUDY

The Data That Changed Everything

Kevin was a financial advisor creating YouTube content about retirement planning. After six months and forty videos, his growth had stalled at around 1,200 subscribers, with videos averaging 400–600 views regardless of topic or effort.

"I was doing everything right," he told me. "Good topics, good thumbnails, consistent posting. But nothing was moving the needle. I didn't know what to change because I didn't know what was broken."

The problem was that Kevin was looking at his analytics wrong. He checked views obsessively, sometimes ten times a day, but never dug into the metrics that actually matter. When we analyzed his data properly, the diagnosis was clear.

His CTR was excellent, averaging 6.2% across his videos. People were clicking his thumbnails. His packaging worked. But his AVD was terrible, averaging just 32%. Viewers were clicking and leaving almost immediately. His content wasn't delivering on what his thumbnails promised.

We dug into his retention graphs. The pattern was consistent across nearly every video: a massive drop in the first 60 seconds, with 40–50% of viewers gone before the one-minute mark. Those who survived past minute one had decent retention, but most never made it that far.

I watched his openings. The problem was immediately obvious. Kevin opened every video with a long, formal introduction. He'd introduce himself, explain his credentials, talk about his firm, mention his years of experience, all before getting to the actual content. By the time he reached the topic viewers clicked for, they'd already left.

We restructured his opening approach with one rule: **the first sentence must deliver value or create curiosity**. Credentials come later, or not at all. His old opening for a Social Security video started:

"Hi, I'm Kevin Matthews with Matthews Financial Advisory. I'm a certified financial planner with over twenty years of experience…"

His new opening:

"Claiming Social Security at the wrong time could cost you over $100,000 in lifetime benefits. I'm going to show you exactly when to claim based on your specific situation."

Same expertise. Same information. Completely different result.

Over 90 days, AVD improved from 32% to 51%. Thirty-second retention jumped from 55% to 78%. Average views per video climbed from 500 to 2,100. Subscribers grew from 1,200 to 4,800. Client inquiries from YouTube went from 1–2 per month to 8–10.

"I spent six months frustrated because I was looking at the wrong number," Kevin reflected. "Views were a symptom, not the disease. The disease was retention, and the cure was my opening. The data told me exactly what to fix. I just wasn't reading it right."

CRAZY SIMPLE ACTION

Your First Analytics Audit

Block 30 minutes. You're establishing your baseline and identifying the single biggest opportunity hiding in your data.

- Open YouTube Studio and record your channel averages for the last 28 days: average CTR, average view duration (both minutes and percentage), average views per video, subscriber conversion per 1,000 views, and total monthly impressions. Write these down. This is your baseline. You'll compare against these numbers monthly to track progress. If your channel is new and you don't have enough data yet, that's fine. Set a reminder to do this audit once you have at least 10 published videos.

- Identify your best and worst performing videos by **AVD**, not by views. Pull up each one and note the CTR, AVD, and total views. Ask yourself honestly: what's different about these two videos? Topic? Hook? Thumbnail style? Structure? Length? This comparison almost always reveals a clear pattern that shows what your audience actually wants versus what you think they want.

- Do a **retention graph deep-dive** on your three most recent videos. For each, note the percentage of viewers remaining at 30 seconds and at the 50% mark. Identify the single biggest drop-off point. Watch that section. Was it boring? Confusing? A tangent?

Once you see the pattern across three videos, you'll know exactly what to fix.

- Based on your findings, identify your **single primary problem**. Is it:

    o CTR problem (people see but don't click → thumbnails and titles need work)

    o Hook problem (people click but leave fast → first 30 seconds need work)

    o Structure problem (people leave mid-video → pacing and pattern interrupts need work)

    o Impressions problem (not enough people seeing videos → consistency is the issue)

Pick one and write it down. That's your focus for the next 30 days. Then schedule your **weekly 15-minute analytics review** as a recurring calendar appointment. Treat it like a client meeting. Data-driven creators outperform gut-feeling creators every single time.

In Chapter 16, we'll explore **YouTube Shorts** and how to use short-form content strategically to accelerate your channel growth without cannibalizing your long-form strategy.

CHAPTER 16
YouTube Shorts: The Strategic Approach for Business Channels

OPENING HOOK

I'm going to tell you about an experiment that cost me a year of my life and taught me everything I needed to know about YouTube Shorts for business channels.

On my @GotCoach channel, I committed to posting one Short every single day for 365 days. No exceptions. No breaks. One vertical video, every day, for an entire year.

The results were fascinating, and probably not what you'd expect.

I gained subscribers. A lot of them, actually. My subscriber count grew faster than it ever had with long-form content alone. Some Shorts went viral, reaching hundreds of thousands of views. On paper, the experiment looked like a massive success.

But here's what the subscriber count didn't show: those new subscribers didn't watch my long-form content. They didn't engage with my channel the way my long-form viewers did. They didn't become leads or clients. They were a different audience entirely, people who wanted 30-second entertainment, not 15-minute educational videos.

When I stopped posting daily Shorts, something interesting happened. My long-form content started performing better. The algorithm seemed relieved. My core audience, the people who actually became clients, remained engaged. The "Shorts subscribers" quietly faded away, never to return.

That experiment taught me a crucial lesson: Shorts are a tool, not a strategy. Used correctly, they can accelerate your growth, introduce new audiences to your content, and repurpose your best ideas for maximum reach. Used incorrectly, they can dilute your brand, attract the wrong audience, and distract you from the content that actually builds your business.

The question isn't whether you should use Shorts. The question is how you should use them, strategically, intentionally, and in service of your actual business goals. This chapter gives you the framework that took me 365 days of painful experimentation to learn.

THE FRAMEWORK

Understanding the Shorts Algorithm

YouTube Shorts operates on a fundamentally different algorithm than long-form content. When you post a Short, YouTube shows it to a small test audience in the vertical, swipeable Shorts feed on mobile. If that test audience engages by watching to completion, liking, commenting, or sharing, YouTube expands distribution to a larger audience. If that larger audience also engages, distribution expands again. This can happen rapidly, with Shorts going from zero to hundreds of thousands of views within hours.

The key metric for Shorts is completion rate, not average view duration. A 30-second Short that 70% of viewers finish will outperform a 60-second Short that only 40% finish. Shorter is generally better for the algorithm.

Here's what most creators don't realize: Shorts viewers and long-form viewers are largely different audiences. Someone scrolling the Shorts feed on their phone during a lunch break is in a completely different mindset than someone who typed a search query and clicked on a 15-minute tutorial. When you gain subscribers from Shorts, many of them will never watch your long-form content. They subscribed for quick hits, not deep dives. This isn't necessarily bad. It just means you need to set realistic expectations about what Shorts can and cannot accomplish for your business.

YouTube has improved the integration between Shorts and long-form over time. Shorts subscribers are more likely to see your long-form content in 2026 than they were a couple of years ago. But the fundamental behavioral divide remains. Someone who discovered you through a 30-second clip while killing time on the bus is a fundamentally different viewer than someone who searched for "how to sell my home in Denver" and chose your 12-minute video. Both have value, but only one is likely to become a client.

When Shorts Help and When They Hurt

Shorts help your business channel in four specific situations:

1. **Trailers for long-form content:** A compelling 30-second clip from your latest video, ending with "full video on my channel," can drive qualified viewers to your deeper content.

2. **Repurposing existing content efficiently:** Taking a powerful 45-second segment from a video you've already filmed costs almost nothing to create.

3. **Testing topics before committing to long-form:** A Short takes minutes to make, and high engagement signals that a full video on that topic would perform well.

4. **Building initial momentum on a new channel:** The Shorts algorithm is more willing to show short content to new audiences than untested long-form.

Shorts hurt your channel when:

- They become your primary content, because you'll build an audience that expects short videos and won't watch your 12-minute content.

- They attract the wrong audience through entertainment-style or trend-chasing content unrelated to your business.

- Time spent creating original Shorts comes at the expense of your long-form content calendar, a bad trade.

- You chase vanity metrics, a Short with 500,000 views that generates zero leads is worth exactly nothing to your business.

I want to be direct about this: I've watched real estate agents destroy perfectly good channels by pivoting to daily Shorts. They get intoxicated by the view counts, which are always dramatically higher than long-form numbers, and gradually shift their time and energy toward short-form content. Six months later, they have impressive vanity metrics and zero business results. Their long-form content withered from neglect, and with it, their lead generation dried up. Don't make that mistake.

The Strategic Shorts Framework

Based on my experiments and client results, here's the framework I recommend for business channels:

- **Maintain a 3-to-4 long-form to 1-to-2 Shorts ratio:** Long-form remains your primary content. Shorts are supplementary, amplifiers, not replacements. If you're publishing twice weekly, that might mean eight long-form videos per month with two to four Shorts mixed in.

- **Repurpose rather than create from scratch:** The most efficient Shorts come from content you've already made. Pull clips from your long-form videos. Turn client FAQ answers into Shorts. Repurpose your best-performing content into vertical format. This maximizes value while minimizing additional time investment.

- **Always bridge back to long-form:** Every Short should serve your broader content strategy. End with a call to action that drives viewers to your full videos, and pin a comment with the link.

- **Stay on brand:** Your Shorts should cover the same topics as your long-form content. If your channel is about real estate, your Shorts should be about real estate, not trending dances or reaction content.

Creating Effective Shorts

The mechanics of a high-performing Short differ from long-form:

- **Length:** Keep it under 40 seconds for optimal completion rates. While Shorts can technically run up to three minutes, shorter Shorts consistently outperform longer ones. Say one thing, say it well, and stop.

- **Hook:** Your first two seconds determine everything. Viewers decide almost instantly whether to keep watching or swipe away. Start with your most compelling statement, never a warm-up or greeting. For example: "The biggest mistake home buyers make..." not "Hey guys, today I want to talk about..."

- **Text on screen:** Many Shorts viewers watch without sound. Adding captions or key text ensures your message lands even when muted. CapCut and Descript both have auto-caption features that make this nearly effortless.

- **Loop potential:** Shorts that people watch multiple times get boosted significantly. Ending your Short in a way that connects back to the beginning, or revealing something that makes viewers want to rewatch, can dramatically boost performance.

The best-performing Shorts I've seen on business channels combine a strong hook, captions, and a loop-worthy ending that makes viewers watch twice before swiping.

The Repurposing Workflow

Creating Shorts from existing content should take 10 to 15 minutes per Short. Here's the process:

As you edit your long-form videos, flag segments that could stand alone, a surprising statistic, a quotable insight, or a compelling 30-second story. These are your Short candidates. Extract the segment, crop to vertical (9:16 aspect ratio) with your face centered, add auto-captions and any relevant text overlays, then optimize the opening so the first two seconds are as strong as possible. You may need to trim the beginning to start at a more compelling moment. At the end, add text or a verbal call to action pointing to your full video, and pin a comment with the link once published.

This workflow means Shorts are essentially a byproduct of your long-form editing process, not a separate production workstream. That's the key to sustainability. The moment you start blocking separate time to brainstorm, film, and edit original Shorts, you've crossed the line from strategic tool to time sink. If a Short can't be created from something you've already made, it probably shouldn't exist on a business channel.

AI INTEGRATION

Your Shorts Content Planner

Use this prompt after completing each long-form video to identify Shorts opportunities from content you've already created.

PROMPT: YouTube Shorts Extraction Planner

Help me identify Shorts opportunities from my long-form content.

- **My niche:** [YOUR INDUSTRY/TOPIC]
- **Recent video topic:** [WHAT THE VIDEO COVERS]
- **Key points covered:** [LIST 3-5 MAIN POINTS]
- **Surprising stats or facts mentioned:** [LIST THEM]
- **Stories or examples shared:** [BRIEFLY DESCRIBE]

Please identify:

1. The 3 best moments to extract as standalone Shorts (with hook suggestions)

2. A compelling opening line for each (first 2 sec)

3. Suggested text overlay for each

4. A bridge CTA for each pointing to the full video

5. Which Short has the highest viral potential and why

Focus on moments that stand alone and make viewers want to see more.

Run this after each long-form video. It takes five minutes to fill out and will identify two to three Shorts you can create from content you've already produced. Over time, you'll develop an instinct for spotting Short-worthy moments while you're still filming.

CASE STUDY

The Right Way to Use Shorts

After my own Shorts experiment, I worked with a real estate agent named Lisa who wanted to incorporate Shorts without making my mistakes.

Lisa had been posting long-form content consistently for about a year. Her channel had grown to 8,000 subscribers, and she was generating 5 to 8 qualified leads per month from YouTube. She'd seen other real estate agents blow up with Shorts and wanted to know if she should add them to her strategy.

"I don't want to chase views for the sake of views," she told me. *"I want to grow my business. Will Shorts actually help with that, or is it just vanity?"*

We designed a strategic approach with clear boundaries:

- Shorts would only come from repurposed long-form content, never created from scratch.

- Maximum two Shorts per week alongside her two long-form videos.

- Every Short had to include a bridge to related long-form content.

- Topics stayed strictly on brand, no trend-chasing.

- The most important rule: track not just views, but whether Shorts viewers actually converted to long-form viewers.

Her workflow was simple. After editing each long-form video, Lisa would identify one or two moments that could stand alone, a surprising market stat, a quick buyer tip, or a compelling neighborhood insight. She'd extract the clip, crop to vertical, add captions using CapCut, and add text at the end saying, *"Full breakdown on my channel."* Total additional time: about 20 minutes per week.

Her best-performing Shorts included:

- *"The one thing that kills home sales"* (pulled from a 14-minute staging video)

- *"This neighborhood is about to explode"* (extracted from a market update)

- *"Why your pre-approval doesn't matter"* (clipped from a buyer mistakes video)

Each one was under 40 seconds and ended with a clear bridge to the full video.

Over six months, her Shorts accumulated about 850,000 total views, with some going modestly viral. She gained approximately 3,200 new subscribers from Shorts. But here's what mattered: long-form views increased 22% because the Shorts were driving traffic back to her full videos. Total subscribers grew from 8,000 to 14,500. Monthly leads climbed from 5–8 up to 12–15. And the total additional time invested was only about 80 minutes per month.

The metric Lisa tracked most closely was what she called *"Shorts-to-long-form conversion."* About 8–12% of Short viewers clicked through to watch more. That proved these weren't empty views.

"The difference from what I've seen other agents do is that I'm not trying to go viral," Lisa reflected. *"A Short with 50,000 views that sends 5,000 people to my full video is worth more than a viral Short with a million views that sends nobody."*

Her advice was perfect: *"Shorts should feel like movie trailers for your real content. They're not the main event. They're the teaser that gets people into the theater."*

CRAZY SIMPLE ACTION

Build Your Shorts Strategy

Block 30 minutes. You're building a Shorts plan that amplifies your long-form strategy rather than distracting from it.

- **Define the role Shorts will play for your channel:** Are they trailers to drive traffic to long-form content? Topic tests before committing to full videos? Momentum builders for a new channel? Or reach extenders for existing content? Pick your primary purpose. Then set your ratio: how many Shorts per long-form video. For most business channels, 1 Short for every 2–3 long-form videos is the right balance.

- **Set your boundaries before you start:** Shorts will only come from repurposed long-form content, not original creation. Set a maximum weekly time budget, 20 to 30 minutes is reasonable. Decide which topics are off-limits to avoid attracting the wrong audience. Write your standard bridge CTA for every Short. These boundaries prevent scope creep from turning Shorts from a supplement into a time sink.

- **Review your last five long-form videos now** and identify the best Short-worthy moment from each. Write down the timestamp and a one-sentence description. This gives you a backlog of five potential Shorts you can create whenever you have a spare 15 minutes. Going forward, flag these moments during editing so they're always ready to extract.

- **Commit to your tracking system:** The only metric that matters for Shorts on a business channel is whether they serve your long-form strategy. Track Shorts-to-long-form conversion by checking whether viewers who find you through Shorts end up watching your full videos. If after 90 days your Shorts are getting views but not driving long-form traffic or generating leads, scale back immediately. Views without business impact are just vanity. The goal is growth, not a dopamine hit from a view counter.

In Chapter 17, we'll explore building your lead generation system, how to turn YouTube viewers into qualified prospects ready to do business with you.

CHAPTER 17
Building Your Lead Generation System

OPENING HOOK

Views don't pay the bills. Subscribers don't pay the bills. Only clients pay the bills.

I've seen creators with 100,000 subscribers struggle to generate leads, and creators with 5,000 subscribers build six-figure businesses entirely from YouTube traffic. The difference isn't audience size, it's whether they've built a system that converts viewers into prospects.

Most business owners approach YouTube like they're building a media company. They chase views. They celebrate subscriber milestones. They measure success by metrics that look impressive in screenshots but don't translate to revenue.

Then they wonder why their channel isn't generating business.

YouTube by itself doesn't generate leads. YouTube generates attention. What you do with that attention, how you capture it, nurture it, and convert it, determines whether your channel becomes a business asset or an expensive hobby.

The creators who generate consistent leads have built what I call a **lead generation system**: a deliberate pathway that guides viewers from casual watcher to qualified prospect. It's not complicated, but it does require intention. You need the right offer, in the right place, with the right call to action, connected to the right follow-up sequence.

I've watched this transformation happen dozens of times. A creator goes from *"I get views but no leads"* to *"I get 15 to 20 qualified inquiries every month"* simply by installing a proper system. Same content. Same audience size. Completely different business results.

When I work with clients, building this system is one of the first things we do, often before they've published a single video. Because without a system to capture leads, even the best content is just entertainment. You might build an audience, but you won't build a business.

This chapter gives you the complete lead generation framework for YouTube-based businesses, from lead magnet to capture page to follow-up sequence, so that every video you publish works to bring you clients.

THE FRAMEWORK

The YouTube Lead Generation Funnel

The path from viewer to client has five stages, and understanding this progression is essential before you build anything.

It starts with a **viewer**: someone watches your video, but you don't know who they are. They're anonymous. Then some become **engaged viewers**, watching multiple videos, subscribing, or commenting. They're showing interest, but you still can't reach them directly.

The critical transition happens when an engaged viewer gives you their contact information, usually an email, in exchange for something valuable. Now they're a **lead**. You can communicate with them outside of YouTube. Through your follow-up, some leads indicate readiness to take action by booking a call, requesting information, or expressing direct interest. They've become **qualified leads**. And finally, some of those hire you or buy from you. They're **clients**.

Your lead generation system's job is to move people smoothly from anonymous viewer to captured lead. Everything beyond that is sales and delivery. Our focus here is that critical bridge between watching your content and raising their hand.

The Lead Magnet: Your Value Exchange

A **lead magnet** is something valuable you give away for free in exchange for contact information. It's the bridge between *anonymous viewer* and *known lead*. And the difference between a lead magnet that converts and one that sits there collecting dust comes down to four qualities:

1. **Solve a specific problem.** "Sign up for my newsletter" converts poorly because there's no clear value. "Download my Home Buyer's 27-Point Checklist" converts well because the viewer

knows exactly what they're getting and why it matters. The more specific the problem, the more qualified the leads.

2. **Deliver immediate value.** Your lead magnet should provide a quick win, something useful they can implement right away. Long courses and extensive guides often go unread. Checklists, templates, and short guides get used.

3. **Directly relate to your paid services.** This naturally attracts only people interested in your area of expertise.

4. **Position you as the expert.** After consuming it, leads should think: "This person clearly knows what they're doing."

The best formats for business channels are checklists ("The Complete Home Staging Checklist"), templates ("My Offer Negotiation Email Templates"), short guides ("The First-Time Buyer's Quick Start Guide"), calculators or tools ("Should You Rent or Buy?"), and video trainings ("Free 20-Minute Masterclass").

Start with one. Many creators make the mistake of building multiple lead magnets before proving one works. Create one high-quality lead magnet, test it, optimize it, and only then consider adding others.

Placement: Where and How to Promote

A great lead magnet is useless if nobody knows about it. You need to promote it in five places, the first is the most important.

1. **Video description.** Your first link should be your lead magnet, not your homepage. The first link gets the most clicks by a wide margin. Use compelling copy: *"FREE: Download my Home Buyer's 27-Point Checklist"* beats a naked URL every time.

2. **Verbal call to action in the video.** This is where most conversions come from. Mention your lead magnet naturally after delivering significant value: *"I go much deeper on this in my free guide. Link in the description if you want the complete checklist."* The best placement for verbal CTAs is mid-video (around 40–60% mark) because it catches viewers who leave before the end. Mention it again at the close, but don't rely solely on the closing since many viewers never make it that far.

3. **Pinned comment.** Pin a comment with your lead magnet offer on every video. It appears at the top of comments and catches viewers who scroll down to engage. Keep it brief and direct.

4. **Channel page description and links section.** Feature your lead magnet prominently for new visitors checking out your channel.

5. **End screen video.** If you have a short landing page video explaining what they'll get, add it as an end screen element on your other videos.

The Capture Page

When someone clicks your link, they land on a **capture page**. This page has one job: get their email address. Everything on the page should serve that single purpose.

- **Headline:** State exactly what they're getting. *"Download Your Free Home Buyer's 27-Point Checklist"* is clear. *"Welcome to My Site"* is not.

- **Benefit bullets:** Three to five bullets explain what they'll learn or gain. Focus on outcomes: *"Never miss a critical inspection item"* beats *"Includes 27 items."*

- **Form:** Keep it simple. Name and email is standard. Every additional field reduces conversions.

- **Visual:** Show a mockup of the lead magnet so the offer feels tangible.

- **Navigation:** Remove all other links. The only action should be opting in. Every other link is a potential exit.

Tools like **Leadpages, ConvertKit, Mailchimp, and Carrd** all work. Even a simple Google Form connected to your email list can get you started. Don't let tool selection become procrastination. A basic page that converts is infinitely better than a fancy page you never finish.

A well-designed capture page should convert **20–40% of visitors**. If yours is under 20%, simplify your page, strengthen your headline, or make the offer more specific. If it's over 40%, you're doing something very right.

The Follow-Up Sequence

Capturing the lead is just the beginning. What happens next determines whether that lead becomes a client. You need a **minimum five-email welcome sequence** that guides new leads from *"just downloaded"* to *"ready to take action."*

Your **first email** goes out immediately and delivers the lead magnet. Thank them, introduce yourself briefly in one or two sentences, and tell them what to expect next.

- **Day 2:** Send a valuable insight related to the lead magnet topic, establishing your expertise with a soft mention of how you help clients.

- **Day 4:** Share a client success story that lets leads envision the transformation.

- **Day 6:** Address a common objection or misconception, building trust through helpfulness.

- **Day 8:** Deliver your direct call to action: an invitation to book a call, schedule a consultation, or take whatever next step makes sense for your business.

After the welcome sequence, move leads to your **regular email communications**, where you continue providing value and making periodic offers. The goal is staying top of mind until they're ready to act. Some leads convert in a week. Others take six months. The sequence ensures you're there when they're ready.

A critical mistake I see constantly: creators build the lead magnet and capture page but never set up the email sequence. They collect emails and then do nothing with them. A list of uncontacted leads is barely better than no list at all. The follow-up is where the actual conversion happens. Without it, you've built **half a bridge.**

AI INTEGRATION

Your Lead Magnet Creator

Use this prompt to develop your lead magnet concept and build your complete system in one session.

PROMPT: Lead Magnet Development

Help me create a high-converting lead magnet for my YouTube channel.

My business: [WHAT YOU DO/SELL]

My target audience: [WHO YOU SERVE]

Their biggest frustration: [MAIN PAIN POINT]

Their desired outcome: [WHAT THEY WANT]

My most popular video topics: [LIST 3–5]

Questions I get asked most: [LIST COMMON Q'S]

Please provide:

1. Three lead magnet concepts (different formats) with compelling titles

2. For each: what it includes and why it appeals

3. Recommendation for which to create first

4. Landing page headline and 5 benefit bullets

5. A verbal CTA script for my videos

6. Subject lines for a five-email welcome sequence

Focus on attracting **qualified prospects likely to become paying clients**, not freebie seekers.

This gives you everything you need to build your lead generation system in one sitting. The key insight is starting with your audience's problems and desires. Lead magnets that address **real pain points** convert far better than generic offerings.

CASE STUDY

From Zero Leads to Sixty Per Quarter

Sandra was a divorce attorney who started a YouTube channel to generate clients. After eight months, she had 3,200 subscribers and averaged 2,000–3,000 views per video. Her content was solid: informative videos about divorce law, property division, and custody issues. Viewers commented. They subscribed.

But she'd gotten **exactly four leads** from YouTube in eight months. Four.

"People watch my videos, they comment, they subscribe," she told me. "But they don't contact me. I know my content is helpful because people tell me so. I just can't figure out how to turn viewers into consultations."

The problem was obvious when I audited her channel: she had **no lead generation system.** Her video descriptions contained her office phone number and a link to her firm's generic website. That was it. No lead magnet. No capture page. No nurture sequence. She was essentially saying: *"Watch my video, then call me if you need a divorce attorney."*

But people going through divorce aren't ready to hire an attorney after watching one video. They need to be educated, nurtured, and guided toward taking action.

We built her **complete system.** The lead magnet was *"The Divorce Preparation Checklist: 15 Things to Do Before Filing,"* which was perfect because it attracted people in the consideration stage, thinking about divorce but not yet ready to hire. These are ideal prospects: early enough to nurture, serious enough to take action.

For placement:

- First link in every video description with compelling copy

- Verbal mentions mid-video and at closing

- Pinned comment on every video

- Updated channel description

The **capture page** was a simple Leadpages template with a clear headline, benefit bullets, a mockup of the checklist, and a two-field form.

The **email sequence** ran five emails over ten days:

1. Deliver the checklist

2. Share insights about the divorce process

3. Tell a client success story

4. Address common fears

5. Invite a free consultation call

Over 90 days, the numbers were staggering:

- 340 lead magnet downloads

- 62 consultation requests (18% conversion from lead to consultation)

- 11 new clients from YouTube

At an average client value of $8,500, that was **$93,500 in revenue** attributed directly to YouTube.

From four leads in eight months to over sixty in three months. Same content. Same audience. The only difference was installing a system to capture and nurture leads.

"I was giving away all this value and then just hoping people would call," Sandra reflected. "Now I understand that hope isn't a strategy. You need to give people a clear next step, make it easy, and stay in touch until they're ready."

Her advice to other professionals: **don't wait until your channel is "big enough" to build a lead system. Build it first.** Sandra wasted eight months of viewers who would have become leads if she'd just given them a way to raise their hand.

CRAZY SIMPLE ACTION

Build Your Lead System This Week

Block 90 minutes. You're building the complete lead generation system that turns your YouTube content into a business asset.

- **15 minutes:** Design your lead magnet. Identify the number one problem your audience wants solved. Decide the quick win you can give them. Choose a format: checklist, template, short guide, calculator, or video training. Write the title. Don't overthink, this first lead magnet won't be your last, but it needs to exist before it can be optimized. Checklists and templates are fastest to create and reliably convert across nearly every niche.

- **30 minutes:** Create your capture page. Write your headline (state exactly what they're getting), 3–5 benefit bullets (focus on outcomes, not features), and set up a simple form requesting name and email. Use any tool you're comfortable with: Leadpages, ConvertKit, Mailchimp, Carrd, or even a Google Form. The design doesn't need to be beautiful, it needs to be live.

- **15 minutes:** Write your standard promotional elements. Create your video description link text (the compelling one-liner above the URL), your verbal CTA script (the mid-video mention you'll use in every video), and your pinned comment template. These three elements get copy-pasted into every video you publish from this point forward. Write them once, reuse forever.

- **30 minutes:** Outline your five-email welcome sequence. For each email, write the subject line and a two-sentence summary.

1. Deliver the lead magnet

2. Share a valuable insight

3. Tell a transformation story

4. Address a common objection

5. Invite them to take the next step

Set a hard deadline: your **entire system goes live within seven days.** Every video you publish without a lead capture system is wasted opportunity. Viewers who would have become leads disappear into the void. Get your system live, even if it's imperfect. You can optimize later. You can't recapture lost viewers.

In Chapter 18, we'll explore converting YouTube leads to clients: the sales conversations and processes that turn qualified prospects into paying customers.

CHAPTER 18
Converting YouTube Leads to Clients

OPENING HOOK

YouTube leads are different. And if you don't understand how they're different, you'll struggle to convert them.

When someone finds you through a Google search or a referral, they're typically in **active buying mode**. They have a problem, they want a solution, and they're evaluating providers. The sales conversation is straightforward: qualify, present, close.

YouTube leads arrive differently. They've been watching you for days, weeks, sometimes months. They've consumed hours of your content. They've heard your stories, absorbed your philosophy, and formed opinions about you as a person. By the time they reach out, they feel like they know you.

This creates a unique dynamic. YouTube leads are often more trusting, more aligned with your approach, and more ready to say yes. The "know, like, trust" factor that normally requires multiple touchpoints has already been built through your content.

But there's a flip side. YouTube leads sometimes arrive with **unrealistic expectations**. They've seen you give away so much value for free that they expect the same in a paid engagement. They might want to skip the consultation and *just get started.* They might assume a personal relationship that doesn't fully exist yet.

Understanding these dynamics is the key to converting YouTube viewers into paying clients. You're not building rapport from scratch, you're deepening rapport that already exists. You're not establishing credibility, you're confirming credibility they've already perceived. You're not convincing them you can help, you're helping them understand **how you'll help in their specific situation.**

I've coached professionals across multiple industries on this exact transition, from real estate agents to financial advisors to attorneys. The patterns are remarkably consistent. Creators who treat YouTube leads like cold prospects leave money on the table. Creators who understand the unique dynamics of these leads and adapt their approach routinely close at **two to three times** the rate of traditional sales conversations.

THE FRAMEWORK

The YouTube Lead Advantage

Before diving into tactics, understand what makes these leads special so you can leverage it.

YouTube leads come **pre-loaded with trust**. By the time someone contacts you, they've likely watched hours of your content. They've seen how you think, heard your voice, observed your expertise. The trust-building phase that normally happens during a sales process has already occurred.

They've also **self-qualified** through your content. If someone has watched multiple videos about first-time home buying, they're probably a first-time buyer. Your content itself filters your audience, so leads who reach out are typically well-matched to your services.

Beyond trust and qualification, your videos communicate not just what you do but **how you think** about what you do. Viewers who resonate with your approach reach out; those who don't go elsewhere. This philosophy alignment means YouTube leads often arrive **pre-sold on your methodology**. And because they've already received value from you for free, skepticism is dramatically reduced compared to cold prospects. They're not wondering if you know what you're talking about, they've seen proof across dozens of videos.

These advantages mean your **close rate on YouTube leads** should be significantly higher than on cold leads, often two to three times higher, but only if you approach the conversation correctly.

The Consultation Framework

Whether you call it a consultation, strategy session, discovery call, or initial meeting, this conversation follows a specific structure that **maximizes conversion** while respecting the relationship you've built.

1. **Acknowledge the YouTube connection (2–3 minutes).**

2. Most consultants skip this, which is a mistake. Ask what videos they watched. What resonated? What questions did the content raise? This honors the relationship they feel they have with you, gives you insight into where they are in their journey, and establishes continuity between your content and the conversation.

3. Example: *"You mentioned you found me through YouTube. I'd love to know what videos you watched and what made you decide to reach out."*

4. **Understand their specific situation (10–15 minutes).**

5. What are they trying to accomplish? What obstacles are they facing? What have they already tried? What does success look like for them? Listen far more than you talk. Your job here is to understand, not to pitch. Ask about their timeline, what's at stake if they don't act, and what has or hasn't worked before. The depth of your questions signals expertise just as much as your answers would.

6. **Bridge their content learnings to their situation (5–7 minutes).**

7. Connect what they've learned from your videos to their case. Reference concepts from your content and show how they apply:

8. *"In that video about staging, I talked about first impressions. In your situation, that principle would mean…"*

9. This demonstrates that you've been listening, shows how your expertise applies, and begins to paint a picture of what working together would accomplish. You're not giving away the complete solution, you're showing you understand the problem and have a path to solve it.

10. **Present the path forward (5–10 minutes).**

11. Be specific about what working together would look like: the process, timeline, expected outcomes, and investment. Don't be vague, vagueness kills conversions.

12. Example: *"Here's what we'd do together in weeks one through four. Here's what clients in similar situations typically achieve. Here's the investment."*

Specificity makes the offer feel real and reduces the anxiety of committing.

13. **Handle questions and close.**

14. After presenting, pause and ask: *"What questions do you have?"* Answer directly. When questions are resolved, ask for the commitment: *"Based on what you've shared, I'm confident we can get you to [outcome]. Are you ready to get started?"* Don't be afraid of the direct ask. YouTube leads have already invested significant time learning from you. If they've booked a call, they're serious. A direct ask respects that seriousness.

I can't stress this enough: the **close is where most professionals choke**. They present beautifully and then trail off, hoping the prospect will volunteer to buy. That almost never happens. You have to ask.

Counterintuitive truth: a confident, direct ask **actually increases trust**. It signals you believe in what you're offering and that it's right for them. Hesitation signals doubt. Confidence signals conviction.

Handling YouTube-Specific Objections

YouTube leads raise objections you won't hear from traditional prospects.

- **"Can't I just watch more videos?"**

- Response: Your videos teach principles and general strategies, but they can't account for the viewer's specific situation. The videos gave them the foundation; working together gives them the application. Think fitness YouTube channel vs. personal trainer, both valuable, completely different experiences.

- **Skipping formalities because they feel they already know you.**

- Acknowledge the warmth, but redirect: there's a difference between knowing your teaching and you knowing their situation. The conversation ensures you can help them effectively.

- **"You give away so much free, why should I pay?"**

- Same analogy: free content helps everyone at a general level. Paid work is about **their specific situation, goals, and your dedicated attention**.

- **"I need to think about it."**

- This often masks a more concrete concern. Ask: *"What specifically do you want to think through? Is it the timing, the investment, or whether this is the right approach?"* Then address the real objection they just revealed.

The Follow-Up System

Not every lead converts on the first call. Many need time, more information, or a change in circumstances before they're ready. A systematic follow-up ensures you don't lose leads who would have converted with patience.

Within 24 hours, send a personalized email: thank them for the conversation, recap what you discussed, reiterate how you can help, include any information they requested, and make the next step clear. This isn't a template blast. Reference specific things they said.

At the one-week mark, send a brief check-in. Share a relevant piece of content, a video, article, or resource, that relates to what you discussed. Don't pressure. Provide value. Through weeks two to four, continue periodic touchpoints: client success stories relevant to their situation, time-sensitive factors if applicable, staying helpful rather than pushy. After that, move unconverted leads to your regular email list and continue providing value through your ongoing content.

The mindset that makes this work: YouTube leads have already demonstrated interest by consuming your content and booking a call. If they don't convert immediately, it's usually about timing, not about you. Your job is to remain available and valuable until the timing is right. Some leads take six months. Some take a year. The follow-up system ensures you're there when they're ready.

AI INTEGRATION

Your Consultation Prep Tool

Use this prompt before every consultation call. Five minutes of preparation dramatically improves your conversion rate.

PROMPT: YouTube Lead Consultation Prep

Help me prepare for a consultation call with a YouTube lead.

My service: [WHAT YOU OFFER]

My typical client: [WHO YOU SERVE BEST]

My service price: [YOUR FEE/PRICING]

About this lead:

Videos they mentioned: [IF KNOWN]

Their inquiry message: [WHAT THEY SAID]

What I know about their situation: [ANY DETAILS]

Please provide:

1. Five tailored discovery questions for their stated situation

2. How to connect my video concepts to their needs

3. Likely objections and specific responses

4. A customized value statement for this lead

5. The ideal next step based on their readiness

Help me enter this call prepared to understand their needs and present a relevant solution. You'll enter conversations prepared rather than reactive, with relevant questions ready and objection responses rehearsed. The five minutes of prep compounds into significantly more closed business over time.

CASE STUDY

The Consultant Who Fixed His Close Rate

Robert was a business consultant generating steady leads from YouTube, about 12 to 15 consultation requests per month. His content was excellent. His lead magnet converted well. But his close rate was stuck at 20%.

"These people reach out saying they love my content," he told me. "They book calls enthusiastically. Then I get on the phone and it's like pulling teeth. Half of them want to just pick my brain. The other half say they need to think about it and I never hear from them again."

When I listened to recordings of his calls, I spotted four problems immediately. First, he skipped the connection phase entirely, jumping straight into discovery questions without acknowledging the YouTube relationship. He treated these calls like cold leads, missing the opportunity to leverage the trust that already existed.

Second, he gave away the solution on the call. When leads described their problems, Robert immediately started solving them for free. By the time he presented his paid services, leads felt like they already had what they needed.

Third, his presentation was vague: "I can help you with your marketing strategy." No specific process, no timeline, no clear outcomes. Leads couldn't visualize what they were buying.

Fourth, he feared the close. He'd present his services and then awkwardly say, "So... let me know what you think." He never actually asked for the commitment.

We rebuilt his consultation with four changes.

New opening: "Before we dive in, what videos of mine did you watch, and what made you decide to book this call?" This immediately activated the pre-built relationship.

New discovery approach: diagnose, don't prescribe. Ask questions that uncover the problem deeply but stop short of providing the complete solution. "I can see exactly what's happening here. Let me show you how we'd fix this if we worked together."

New presentation: specific and visual. "Here's our process: Week 1 we do X, Week 2 we do Y, by Week 4 you'll have Z. Most clients see [specific outcome] within 60 days. The investment is [price]."

New close: simple and direct. "Based on what you've shared, I'm confident we can achieve [outcome] for you. Are you ready to get started?"

After 60 days, his close rate jumped from 20% to 48%. "Brain picker" calls dropped from roughly 40% to about 10%. The "need to think about it" responses now converted 35% through his follow-up system. Average consultation length shortened from 45 minutes to 32 minutes because calls were more focused. Monthly revenue roughly doubled from the same lead volume.

"The biggest shift was realizing that YouTube leads aren't strangers," Robert reflected. "They already trust me. My job isn't to prove myself. It's to understand their situation and show them the path forward. When I stopped treating consultations like auditions and started treating them like conversations with people who already wanted to work with me, everything changed."

CRAZY SIMPLE ACTION

Optimize Your Sales Conversation

Block 45 minutes. You're building the consultation framework that turns YouTube attention into revenue.

- Spend 10 minutes honestly auditing your current approach. Estimate your close rate. What's the most common reason leads don't convert? Do you currently acknowledge the YouTube connection at the start? Do you ask discovery questions before presenting solutions? Do you diagnose without giving away the complete solution? Do you present a specific process, timeline, and outcomes? Do you directly ask for the commitment? Do you follow up systematically? Be brutally honest. The gaps you identify here are the revenue you're leaving on the table.

- Spend 15 minutes scripting your consultation framework. Write your opening question that acknowledges YouTube. Write your five best discovery questions. Write your bridge statement that connects your content to their situation. Outline your presentation with the specific process, timeline, outcomes, and investment. Write your closing question. You're not memorizing a script. You're building a framework so you never enter a call unprepared.

- Spend 10 minutes preparing objection responses. Write your response to "I need to think about it" (ask what specifically they want to think through). Write your response to "Can't I just watch more videos?" (fitness channel versus personal trainer). Write your response to "That's more than I expected" (anchor to the value of the outcome, not the cost of the service). Rehearse these out loud until they feel natural, not scripted.

- Spend 10 minutes building your follow-up sequence. Write the outline for your 24-hour follow-up email. Plan your week-one check-in approach. Decide your long-term nurture plan for leads who don't convert immediately. Then commit to executing this framework on your very next consultation call. Every unconverted YouTube lead represents hours of content they watched, trust you built, and attention you earned. Don't waste that investment with an unfocused conversation. Follow the framework, ask for the commitment, and follow up systematically.

In Chapter 19, we'll explore **building your YouTube team**: when to hire help, what to delegate first, and how to scale beyond what you can do alone.

CHAPTER 19
Building Your YouTube Team

OPENING HOOK

There's a ceiling every YouTube creator hits. You're doing everything yourself: researching topics, writing scripts, filming, editing, creating thumbnails, writing descriptions, managing comments, promoting on social media. You've gotten efficient. You've batched your work. But there are still only so many hours in a week.

You want to publish more frequently, but you can't. You want to improve production quality, but you don't have time to learn advanced editing. You want to respond to every comment and nurture your community, but engagement falls through the cracks when client work picks up.

This is the scaling wall. And most creators respond in one of two ways.

Some accept the ceiling as permanent. They settle into a sustainable but limited rhythm, never growing beyond what one person can manage. Others try to scale too fast. They hire help before they have systems, bringing on team members who don't understand the vision and can't replicate the quality. Wasted money, inconsistent content, frustration for everyone.

There's a better path: strategic scaling. Building a team methodically, starting with the right role, at the right time, with the right systems in place.

I run a YouTube management company where our team handles everything except recording for our clients. I've learned firsthand which tasks delegate effectively and which require more oversight. I've also watched dozens of clients scale their own channels. Some successfully. Some disastrously. The pattern is consistent: creators who scale successfully do so incrementally, with clear systems and communication. Creators who fail try to hand off everything at once to someone who doesn't understand their brand.

THE FRAMEWORK

When You're Ready to Scale

Not every creator should hire help. Scaling too early wastes money and creates problems you're not ready to manage. You're ready when several conditions are true simultaneously.

Your channel needs to be generating revenue, whether from client acquisition, AdSense, sponsorships, or products. YouTube should be paying for itself before you add expenses. Hiring before revenue is gambling. Hiring after revenue is investing.

You also need a proven content system: you know what topics work, you know your filming process, you know your editing style. If you're still experimenting with what your channel should be, it's too early to bring in help. They can't replicate something that doesn't exist yet.

Your bottleneck should be time, not knowledge. If you could work more hours, you'd create more content and grow faster. You're not stuck because you don't know what to do. You're stuck because you can't do it all. That's a scalable problem. You need to be able to articulate your brand and standards clearly enough to teach them. Could you explain your channel's voice to someone else? Do you know what makes a thumbnail "yours" versus generic? If these are clear in your head, they can be taught.

And here's the one most people skip: you have to be willing to manage. Hiring isn't a magic solution. You'll spend time training, reviewing work, giving feedback, and communicating. If you hate the idea of managing, scaling will feel like trading one burden for another.

The Scaling Sequence

When you're ready, the sequence matters. Start with the role that gives you the highest leverage: the most time back for the least management overhead.

Your first hire should be a video editor. For most creators, editing is the biggest time sink, three to five hours per video. It's teachable because your style can be documented and replicated. Quality is visible and easy to review before anything goes live. And it doesn't require your voice or expertise, just technical skill. Your editor handles rough cuts, jump cuts, B-roll insertion, graphics, captions, color correction, audio cleanup, and final export. Initially, you'll review everything closely. Over time, they'll need less oversight.

Your second hire should be a thumbnail designer. Once editing is handled, thumbnails become the next leverage point. They have massive impact on performance since CTR determines reach. Design is a specialized skill where a good designer actually improves quality, not just saves time. And review is quick: you can approve or request changes in minutes. Your designer creates concepts, executes designs, tests variations, and maintains brand consistency across your catalog.

Your third hire is a content manager or virtual assistant. When editing and thumbnails are covered, administrative tasks become the bottleneck: writing descriptions and metadata, scheduling and publishing videos, responding to comments, managing your content calendar, repurposing content for other platforms, and basic analytics tracking. Advanced hires like scriptwriters, videographers, or strategists come later, if at all. Most business YouTube channels can scale significantly with just these first three roles.

Finding and Vetting Candidates

For editors, look at Upwork and Fiverr for freelancers (wide range of quality and price), YouTube editor communities and Discord servers, referrals from other creators, and local film students.

For thumbnail designers, try specialized YouTube thumbnail services, graphic design freelancers with YouTube portfolio work, and design communities like Dribbble or Behance.

For content managers, virtual assistant agencies, online job boards like Indeed and LinkedIn, and referrals from your business network.

The vetting process should follow four steps regardless of role:

1. Review their portfolio for work similar to what you need.

2. Give them a paid test project before committing. Emphasize paid. Edit one video. Design three thumbnails. This reveals actual skill and working style without exploiting anyone's time.

3. Evaluate their communication during the test. Are they responsive? Do they ask clarifying questions? Do they hit deadlines? Communication issues rarely improve after hiring.

4. Start with a 30-day trial before any long-term commitment. This gives both sides an exit if the fit isn't right.

Systems Before People

Hiring without systems creates chaos. I cannot stress this enough. Before bringing someone on, you need documentation in place.

A style guide shows your visual and tonal preferences. For editors, this means pacing examples, transition preferences, graphic styles, and music guidelines. For designers, it means color palette, font choices, layout templates, and examples of work you love and hate.

A process document provides step-by-step instructions for how work flows: where raw files go, what the review process looks like, how revisions are requested, what "done" looks like. The clearer the process, the less confusion and back-and-forth.

You need a communication protocol defining where you talk (Slack, email, project management tool), how quickly messages should be answered, and when check-ins happen. You need an organized shared drive where footage, graphics, music, and finished files live in consistent locations. When your editor knows exactly where to find B-roll and exactly where to deliver the final cut, everything moves faster.

And you need a feedback framework. I recommend the "specific plus solution" approach: instead of "I don't like this," say "The text is hard to read. Try increasing the size by 20% and adding a drop shadow." Clear, actionable feedback accelerates improvement. Vague feedback creates frustration and repeated mistakes.

Managing Without Micromanaging

The goal of scaling is to free up your time, not trade production work for management work.

Front-load your training investment. The first few weeks should be intensive: review everything closely, give detailed feedback, and be available for questions. This pays off fast as your team member learns your standards and needs less oversight. After that initial period, shift to review checkpoints rather than constant check-ins. For editing, review the rough cut and then the final. For thumbnails, review concepts and then final designs. This maintains quality control without constant monitoring.

When you find yourself giving the same feedback repeatedly, add it to your style guide. The goal is to build a reference document that answers questions before they're asked. As your team proves reliable, reduce review intensity gradually. But never stop reviewing entirely. Watch every video before it goes live. Look at every thumbnail. Your name is on the content, and final quality is always your responsibility.

And celebrate wins. When a video performs well, acknowledge the team's contribution. When viewers mention production quality, share the feedback. People do better work when they feel valued. That's not soft management advice, that's a retention strategy. Losing a trained team member and starting over costs far more than a kind word and an occasional bonus.

AI INTEGRATION

Your Team Documentation Builder

Use this prompt to create the documentation you need before hiring. This generates roughly 80% of what you'll need in one session.

PROMPT: YouTube Team Documentation Creator

Help me create onboarding documentation for a new team member on my YouTube channel.

Role: [EDITOR / THUMBNAIL DESIGNER / VA]

My channel niche: [YOUR TOPIC/INDUSTRY]

My brand voice: [DESCRIBE YOUR TONE AND STYLE]

My visual style: [DESCRIBE YOUR AESTHETIC]

Examples of my best work: [DESCRIBE 2-3 VIDEOS]

What makes those great: [WHAT YOU LIKE ABOUT THEM]

Things to avoid: [PET PEEVES, STYLE NO-NOS]

Please create:

1. A style guide specific to this role

2. A step-by-step process workflow

3. A pre-submission checklist they can self-review

4. Five common mistakes to avoid for this role

5. Three paid test project ideas for candidates

6. A template for giving constructive feedback

Make documentation clear enough that someone new could follow it without extensive hand-holding. Refine the output based on your specific preferences, then use it as your onboarding foundation. Good documentation is the difference between a team member who succeeds and one who struggles. Update it continuously as you discover gaps.

CASE STUDY

From Solo Creator to Small Team

Amanda was a business coach with a thriving YouTube channel: 12,000 subscribers, consistent leads, and content her audience loved. But she was drowning in production work.

"I was spending 15 to 20 hours a week on YouTube," she told me. "Filming was maybe two hours. The rest was editing, thumbnails, descriptions, posting, responding to comments. I couldn't grow my coaching practice because YouTube ate all my time. But YouTube was generating my clients, so I couldn't stop."

She'd tried hiring before. A freelance editor from Fiverr. "It was a disaster. I'd send him footage and get back something that looked nothing like my channel. Wrong music, wrong pacing, wrong graphics. I spent more time fixing his work than I would have spent editing myself."

The problem wasn't the editor. The problem was Amanda hadn't prepared to delegate. She had no style guide, no process documentation, no clear instructions. She expected the editor to read her mind.

We started over with a systematic approach. Before hiring anyone new, Amanda spent a weekend creating her style guide. She recorded a

Loom video showing how she edited and explaining her choices. She created a folder of example edits, good and bad, with annotations. She wrote out her complete process from raw footage to published video. Only then did she post in a YouTube creator community with her specific requirements and budget.

She received fifteen applications, reviewed portfolios, and selected three for paid test projects. Each finalist edited the same raw video following Amanda's style guide. Two delivered work that missed the mark. One, Maria, nailed it. Not perfect, but close. And Maria asked smart questions during the process, showing she understood the importance of matching Amanda's style.

Amanda committed to intensive oversight for the first month. She reviewed Maria's rough cuts with detailed feedback. She updated her style guide when she found gaps. By week four, Maria's edits needed only minor tweaks. Three months later, with editing handled, Amanda hired a thumbnail designer using the same process: documentation first, test project, training period. Then a part-time VA for descriptions, scheduling, and comment management.

The results after six months were dramatic. Amanda's YouTube time dropped from 15–20 hours per week down to 4–5 hours. Publishing frequency doubled from once to twice per week. Production quality actually improved because Maria was a better editor than Amanda. Subscribers grew from 12,000 to 24,000. Coaching revenue roughly doubled because she had more time for client work. Her monthly team cost was approximately $1,800. The revenue generated by the freed-up time was approximately $8,000 per month.

"The first time I tried to hire, I was trying to save time," Amanda reflected. "The second time, I was trying to build a system. The difference was everything. Now my team runs the machine. I just show up, record, and review. It's the best investment I've ever made in my business."

CRAZY SIMPLE ACTION

Prepare to Scale

Block 45 minutes. Whether you're ready to hire now or six months from now, this preparation work needs to happen first.

- Spend 10 minutes on an honest readiness assessment. Is your channel generating revenue? Do you have a proven content system you've used for at least three months? Is your bottleneck time rather than knowledge? Can you articulate your brand voice and visual style clearly enough to teach them? Are you willing to invest time in training and management? If four or five of these are true, you're ready. If fewer, focus on building your foundation first and revisit this chapter when the conditions change.

- Identify your first hire by tracking where your time actually goes. For one week, log how many hours you spend on each YouTube task: planning, filming, editing, thumbnails, descriptions, comments, promotion. The task that eats the most time without requiring your voice or expertise is your first hire. For most creators, that's editing. But let the data confirm it rather than assuming.

- Spend 20 minutes starting your documentation. You don't need everything finished today, but start your style guide with three elements: two or three example videos that represent your quality standard, a list of things you definitely don't want (pet peeves, style choices that feel wrong for your brand), and your process from raw footage to published video written as sequential steps. This document will grow over time, but having even a basic version puts you ahead of 90% of creators who hire with zero documentation.

- Design your paid test project. Write down exactly what you'll ask candidates to do, what you'll pay for the test (always pay for test work), what success looks like specifically, and what red flags would disqualify someone. Then set a timeline: documentation complete by a specific date, job posting live by a specific date, test projects completed by a specific date, first team member starting by a specific date. Scaling is an investment of both money and time to build systems. Done right, it multiplies your impact while freeing you to focus on what only you can do: being the face and voice of your brand.

In Chapter 20, we'll address the psychological game: staying motivated through slow growth, handling criticism, and building the mental resilience required for long-term YouTube success.

CHAPTER 20
The Mental Game: Psychology and Resilience for Creators

OPENING HOOK

Nobody talks about the crying.

I mean that literally. In all the YouTube advice content you've consumed, nobody has told you about the night you'll stare at a video you spent eight hours creating and watch it sit at 43 views for a week. Nobody warned you about the comment from a stranger telling you you're terrible at this, and how it will echo in your head louder than a hundred compliments. Nobody mentioned the specific kind of loneliness that comes from putting your face, voice, and ideas into the world and hearing nothing back.

I've been there. Multiple times.

Early in the @VanLife journey, there was a stretch of about three months where I questioned everything. Growth had stalled. A handful of negative comments had gotten under my skin more than I wanted to admit. I watched competitors with flashier production explode past me while I ground out videos that felt invisible. My wife could tell I was wearing down because I'd go quiet after checking analytics. I started filming less. Started finding excuses not to set up the camera.

I didn't quit. But I came close. And when I talk to the creators I coach, I hear the same story over and over. The technical challenges are learnable. The strategy is deployable. But the psychological game is where most channels actually die.

The skills in this chapter won't show up in your analytics. There's no metric for mental resilience. But I guarantee this: the creators who reach 10,000 subscribers aren't necessarily more talented or more strategic than those who quit at 200. They're tougher. They've learned to manage their own psychology. And that's a skill you can build just like any other.

THE FRAMEWORK

The Five Psychological Traps

Understanding the traps is how you avoid them. These aren't random feelings, they're predictable patterns that hit nearly every creator at predictable moments.

The Comparison Spiral. You find a channel in your niche that started after you. They have more subscribers. Their thumbnails look cleaner. Their comments section is buzzing. Something hot and uncomfortable starts building in your chest, and suddenly every video you've made looks amateurish. This spiral is poisonous because it distorts reality. You're comparing your behind-the-scenes to their highlight reel. You're seeing their best-performing videos, not the twenty duds they posted before their breakout. And you're comparing at a snapshot in time rather than looking at trajectories. The creator who looks unstoppable today probably had a miserable first year too.

The Vanity Metric Trap. We covered the right metrics in Chapter 15, but knowing which numbers matter and actually internalizing them are different things. Your brain is wired to fixate on subscriber counts and view totals because those are visible, public numbers. They feel like verdicts on your worth. A video that gets 200 views feels like a failure, even if your lead magnet got 15 downloads from it and three became clients. That's a spectacular result for a business channel, but your brain doesn't see it that way because the view count felt small.

Imposter Syndrome. You're six months in. You've published 30 videos. Someone leaves a comment: "Thank you so much, this changed how I approach my business." And instead of feeling proud, your first thought is: "If they knew how little I actually know…" This one is sneaky because it intensifies the more successful you get. Every new milestone raises the stakes. Every new subscriber is another person you might disappoint. The antidote is remembering that you don't need to know everything. You just need to know more than the person watching. And if you've been in your industry for years, you know infinitely more than someone starting from zero.

The Perfectionism Prison. This is imposter syndrome's overachieving cousin. You won't publish until the video is perfect. The thumbnail needs one more tweak. The script needs one more revision. The audio sounds a little off in that one section. Perfectionism masquerades as having high standards, but it's actually fear of judgment dressed up in productive clothing. Every hour you spend polishing a video that's already good enough is an hour you're not spending creating the next one. And on YouTube, volume and consistency beat perfection every single time.

Burnout. This one creeps up quietly. You start dreading filming day. The content calendar feels like a prison sentence. You resent the camera. You fantasize about deleting your channel and never making another video. Burnout doesn't come from working hard. It comes from working hard without seeing progress, or working hard without replenishing your energy. The batching system from Chapter 14 helps prevent it, but burnout is ultimately a signal that something in your approach needs to change, not that you should quit.

Building Your Psychological Toolkit

The creators who survive the mental game don't have thicker skin or more willpower. They have systems for managing their psychology, the same way they have systems for filming and editing.

Evidence Journal. When negative thoughts spiral, your brain ignores contradicting evidence. An Evidence Journal is a running document where you record every win, no matter how small: a kind comment, a lead that mentioned your video, a retention number that improved, a subscriber milestone. When the dark days come, and they will, you open this journal and let the evidence override the emotion. I keep mine in a note on my phone. It has entries like: "Viewer DM: watched 14 videos before calling, hired me on first meeting." That one entry has pulled me out of a funk more than once.

Strict Analytics Schedule. Checking analytics multiple times a day is an anxiety machine. Set one day per week for your 15-minute review from Chapter 15 and do not open YouTube Studio outside that window. Turn off the YouTube Studio app notifications. Seriously. Compulsive checking isn't giving you actionable information, it's feeding your insecurity. One client told me that moving from daily analytics checks to weekly checks was the single most impactful change she made for her mental health as a creator.

Creator Support Network. YouTube creation, especially for business owners, is isolating. Your spouse doesn't fully get it. Your friends wonder why you're "playing internet" instead of running your business. Find two to three other creators at a similar stage and check in regularly. Share wins. Vent frustrations. Celebrate milestones together. This doesn't need to be a formal mastermind, a group chat with two creators you trust can make a massive difference.

Separate Identity from Channel. This is the hardest one. When a video underperforms, it feels personal because you are the content. Your face, your voice, your ideas. But a video's performance is the result of dozens of variables, many of which have nothing to do with you: the algorithm's mood, timing, thumbnail performance, search competition that week. A video that gets 200 views isn't a statement about your worth, it's data about one piece of content's performance under a specific set of conditions.

Handling Negative Comments and Criticism

If you create content long enough, someone will say something cruel about it. Probably many someone's. Here's a framework that protects your mental state without numbing you to legitimate feedback.

First, recognize the three types of negative comments.

Constructive criticism sounds like: "The audio was hard to hear in this one," or "I wish you'd gone deeper on that second point." This is gold. It hurts briefly and then makes you better.

Trolling sounds like: "This is the dumbest video I've ever seen," or personal attacks on your appearance, voice, or intelligence. This is noise from people who will never be your audience.

Projection sounds like: "Must be nice to have time to make videos," or "Easy for you to say." These comments say everything about the commenter and nothing about you.

Constructive criticism gets a genuine thank-you and consideration. Trolling gets deleted or ignored, never engagement.

Projection gets internal compassion and external silence. The mistake most creators make is responding to trolls, which feeds the cycle. Delete, block if necessary, and move on. One negative comment can feel like the dominant opinion, but it never is. For every person who comments something cruel, there are dozens who watched, valued what you created, and simply moved on without saying anything.

The Long Game Mindset

YouTube growth is not linear. It's exponential, which means it feels painfully slow at first and then shockingly fast later. Your first 1,000 subscribers might take six months. Your next 1,000 might take six weeks. But you'll never reach the fast part if you quit during the slow part.

I tell every creator I work with the same thing: commit to 100 videos before you evaluate whether YouTube is working. Not 10. Not 30. One hundred. Because the compounding effect that makes YouTube so powerful takes time to build. Your first 50 videos train the algorithm, build your library, develop your skills, and establish your presence. Your next 50 are where the return on that investment starts showing up.

Think about it this way: every video you publish is a permanent asset in a searchable library. Video 47 might be the one that catches the algorithm. Video 62 might be the one a future client watches that makes them call you. You don't know which video will be the breakthrough, so the only losing strategy is to stop making them.

AI INTEGRATION

Your Creator Mindset Coach

Use this prompt when you're in a creative rut, feeling discouraged, or considering quitting. Sometimes an outside perspective, even from AI, can reframe the situation.

PROMPT: YouTube Creator Mindset Reset

I'm a YouTube creator feeling discouraged.

Help me get perspective.

- My channel niche: [YOUR TOPIC]
- How long I've been creating: [MONTHS/YEARS]

- Current subscriber count: [NUMBER]

- Videos published: [NUMBER]

- What's discouraging me specifically: [DESCRIBE]

Please provide:

1. Honest perspective on my progress compared to typical channels in this niche and timeframe

2. Three things I should be proud of based on what I've described

3. The one adjustment most likely to change my trajectory

4. A realistic expectation for where I'll be in 6 months if I stay consistent

5. A reminder of why I started and why it matters

Be honest but encouraging. Don't sugarcoat, but help me see what I might be missing.

This isn't a replacement for your creator support network. But when it's 11 PM and you're staring at analytics that make you want to quit, having a structured way to process those feelings can keep you from making an emotional decision you'll regret.

CASE STUDY

The Creator Who Almost Walked Away

Leah Courage is a real estate agent in Washington State who started her YouTube channel with tremendous energy. She filmed twice a week, built a content calendar, optimized her thumbnails. All the technical boxes were checked.

At the four-month mark, she had 280 subscribers and videos averaging 150 views. Objectively, that's decent progress for a new business channel in a mid-sized market. Subjectively, Leah was devastated.

"I compared myself to everyone," she told me. "There was another agent in my market with 3,000 subscribers who started around the same time. I'd watch his videos and think, 'What does he have that I don't?' I started second-guessing everything, my topics, my style, my whole approach. I'd film a video, watch it back, and convince myself it wasn't good enough to publish. I had six finished videos sitting on my hard drive that never went live."

The comparison spiral triggered perfectionism, which triggered a publishing slowdown, which triggered stalled growth, which triggered more comparison. She was trapped in a reinforcing loop that was killing her channel.

We addressed it on three fronts.

1. **Evidence Journal.** She resisted at first, calling it "cheesy." But within two weeks, she had logged four leads that came directly from YouTube, two of which became clients. The journal didn't change her metrics, it changed what she noticed about her metrics.

2. **Analytics boundaries.** She deleted the YouTube Studio app from her phone and committed to a Wednesday-only analytics review. "I realized I was checking 10 to 15 times a day," she admitted. "That's not analysis. That's anxiety."

3. **Comparison management.** We reviewed a competitor's channel analytics through Social Blade. His subscriber count was higher, yes. But his view-to-subscriber ratio was lower, his content less niche-focused, and he wasn't generating leads because he had no lead system. Leah was actually outperforming him in every metric that mattered for business results, she just couldn't see it because she was fixated on the one number that didn't matter most.

Over the following six months, Leah published the six videos she'd been hoarding plus 40 more. Her channel grew to 2,800 subscribers. Her lead generation system brought in 8–12 qualified leads per month. She closed 14 transactions sourced from YouTube, totaling over $180,000 in commissions.

"The mental game was the real battle," Leah said. "Once I got my head right, the tactics I'd already learned started working. The strategy was always solid. My psychology was the bottleneck."

CRAZY SIMPLE ACTION

Build Your Resilience System

Block 20 minutes. You're building the psychological infrastructure that keeps you creating when your brain tells you to stop.

- **Start your Evidence Journal** right now. Open a note on your phone or a fresh document titled "YouTube Wins." Write down every positive result from your YouTube journey so far, no matter how small. A kind comment, a lead, a skill you've improved, a video you're proud of. If you haven't started yet, write down why you started and the specific outcome you're working toward. Commit to adding at least one entry per week going forward.

- **Set your analytics boundaries.** Delete the YouTube Studio app from your phone if you're a compulsive checker. Pick one day and time for a weekly 15-minute review and put it on your calendar as a recurring appointment. Outside that window, don't check. This isn't about ignoring data, it's about consuming data on your terms instead of letting it consume you.

- **Identify your creator support network.** Write down two to three people who are also creating content or building something publicly. They don't need to be in your niche or even on YouTube, they just need to understand the emotional experience of putting yourself out there. Reach out to at least one this week. If you can't think of anyone, join a creator community: Aaron's Skool group, a Facebook group for YouTube creators, a local business owners group. Isolation is a resilience killer.

- **Make your 100-video commitment.** Write this down where you'll see it daily: "I commit to publishing 100 videos before I evaluate whether YouTube is working for my business." Sticky note it near your camera, set it as your phone wallpaper, whatever it takes to keep this commitment front and center on the days when 100 feels impossible. The creators who win aren't the ones who never feel discouraged, they're the ones who keep creating anyway.

In Chapter 21, we'll explore the AI tools and automation that can dramatically reduce your production time, letting you create more

content with less effort so you can sustain this commitment for the long
haul.

CHAPTER 21
Building Your YouTube Community: From Viewers to Advocates

OPENING HOOK

I knew something had shifted on my @VanLife channel when I posted a video about a custom Sprinter build and a guy named Steve left a comment within four minutes. Not a generic "great video" comment. Steve wrote three paragraphs about how my approach to the electrical system differed from what he'd seen on other channels, asked a follow-up question about lithium batteries, and tagged two friends planning their own builds.

I recognized Steve's name because he'd been commenting for months. Same with a handful of other regulars. These people showed up every single upload. They answered other viewers' questions before I could get to them. When someone left a snarky comment about my editing style, three regulars jumped in and defended the channel before I even saw the notification.

That's not an audience. That's a community.

And the difference matters more than most creators realize. An audience watches your content. A community creates momentum around it. An audience might eventually buy from you. A community sells for you without being asked because they feel ownership in what you're building.

I've coached real estate agents with 15,000 subscribers who can't generate a single lead, and agents with 2,000 subscribers who close deals every month from YouTube. The difference is always the same. The bigger channel has viewers. The smaller channel has a community. The viewers scroll past. The community shares videos in Facebook groups, recommends the agent to friends at dinner parties, and DMs potential clients saying, "You need to watch this person's channel."

You can't buy that. You can't fake it. But you can absolutely build it. And it doesn't require being online 14 hours a day responding to every comment with a novel. It requires strategy, consistency, and understanding what actually makes people feel like they belong.

THE FRAMEWORK

Why Community Beats Subscriber Count Every Time

Let me give you the business case first, because I know some of you are thinking this sounds like soft, feel-good advice that doesn't move the needle.

YouTube's algorithm rewards engagement signals: comments, likes, shares, and return viewers. A channel with 3,000 subscribers and an engaged community generates more of those signals per video than a channel with 30,000 passive followers. The algorithm doesn't care about your subscriber count, it cares about what happens when you publish. If your community shows up within the first hour, comments, and watches the whole video, YouTube takes notice and starts pushing that content to new audiences.

Then there's the trust factor. When a potential client lands on your channel and sees 40 comments from real people praising your advice, sharing their results, and having genuine conversations, that's social proof you couldn't buy with a marketing budget. Those comments do more selling than your video description ever will.

Community also makes your channel resilient. Every creator has videos that underperform. If you have no community, a bad video means crickets. If you have a community, even your worst video gets a baseline of engagement that keeps the algorithm interested. Your floor goes up. That's a huge deal when you're trying to build consistency.

And the referral effect is where it gets really interesting. Your most engaged community members become an unpaid marketing team. They share your videos in online forums. They mention you in conversations. They tag friends. On my @GotCoach channel, I can trace at least 30% of new subscriber growth to community members actively recommending the channel to people in their networks. I never asked them to do that, they just did it because they felt connected to what we were building.

Comments Are Where Community Lives or Dies

Your comment section is either building community or killing it. There's no neutral. And most creators accidentally choose the second option because they treat comments as an afterthought.

Respond to every comment in the first 24 hours. This is the most important window. Your earliest commenters are your most engaged viewers. They watched quickly and felt compelled to interact. If you respond within that window with something substantial, you're telling them their participation matters. If you ignore them for three days, you're telling them it doesn't.

And I mean respond with substance. "Thanks!" is better than silence, but it's lazy. "Thanks! That's a great point. I actually covered the permitting side of this in my video on [topic], might be worth checking out" creates real connection. You're adding value, extending the conversation, and giving that person a reason to come back.

When someone shares their situation in a comment, ask a follow-up question. "That's a tough spot. What have you tried so far?" turns a dead-end comment into a conversation thread other viewers read and engage with. Now your comment section looks alive instead of like a graveyard of thumbs-up emojis.

Pin comments strategically, not your own promotional stuff. Pin a comment from a viewer who shared a great resource, answered someone else's question, or posted a genuine testimonial about your content. This rewards your most engaged people and shows everyone else what kind of participation gets recognized.

Negative comments are where most creators panic. Here's the filter: trolls seeking attention get deleted or ignored. Genuine criticism or skepticism gets a thoughtful response. When you respond graciously to someone who disagrees, your community watches that interaction closely. Handle it well, and you often convert the critic into a fan while showing everyone else that this is a channel run by someone with confidence and class.

Creating Reasons for People to Participate

Community doesn't build itself. You have to create specific, intentional opportunities for people to engage. This is where most business channels completely drop the ball.

End every video with a real question. Not "What do you think?" because that's too vague and nobody answers vague questions. Try, "What's the one neighborhood in your city that's undervalued right now? Drop it in the comments, I read every single one." Specificity matters. The promise that you actually read comments matters more.

When someone asks a killer question in your comments, turn it into a video. And when you do, say their name: "This video was inspired by a question from [username] in the comments of my last video." Watch what happens. That person becomes a superfan overnight. Every other commenter starts putting more thought into their questions because they want to be featured too.

Once you hit 500 subscribers, you unlock the Community tab. Most creators either ignore it or use it to spam links to their latest video. Both are wrong. The Community tab is for building connection between uploads. Post polls about industry topics. Share behind-the-scenes photos of your filming setup. Drop quick tips that are too short for a full video. Ask what content your audience wants next. Two to three posts a week keeps you visible without overwhelming feeds.

Celebrate wins publicly. When a viewer comments that they closed a deal, got a promotion, or solved a problem your video addressed, make a big deal out of it. A "Congratulations, that's awesome!" plus a heart doesn't cost anything, but it creates a moment that person remembers. It also signals to everyone watching that this channel is a place where people succeed together.

Building a Shared Identity

The communities that stick have something beyond just watching the same channel. They have a sense of *we*.

Start by defining who your people are. Not your target demographic, your tribe. Are they "first-time homebuyers tired of getting bad advice"? "Service pros who refuse to cold call anymore"? "Agents building real businesses, not chasing transactions"? Give them an identity they can claim.

Use *we* and *us* instead of *you* and *I* when you're teaching. "As business owners, we know that cold calling is a grind" hits differently than "As a business owner, you know that cold calling is a grind." One puts you on a stage as the teacher. The other puts you in the trenches together.

Create shared language. When you have frameworks, terms, or phrases unique to your channel, they become markers of belonging. On @GotCoach, when someone references one of my frameworks in a comment, I know they're not a casual viewer, they're a community member. And I make sure they know I noticed.

Be clear about what your channel stands for, not just the information you share, but the values behind it. For me, it's no-fluff, tactical, actually deployable advice. When I say "keep it crazy simple," that's not just a catchphrase. It's a filter that attracts people who value substance over hype and repels those who want shortcuts. That self-selection is exactly what you want.

Making This Sustainable

I can already hear some of you thinking: "Aaron, I barely have time to make videos. Now you want me to manage a community too?"

Here's how you do it without losing your mind.

Set engagement windows. Instead of checking comments all day like you're refreshing a dating app, pick two slots. Maybe 15 minutes in the morning, 15 minutes in the evening. Batch your engagement the same way you batch your filming. Get in, respond with intention, get out.

Not all comments need the same level of response. Questions get thorough answers. Positive feedback gets acknowledgment. Generic "great video" comments get a heart. Trolls get nothing. Learn to triage and you'll cut engagement time in half while actually improving the quality of your responses.

As your channel grows, delegate some of this to your content manager (see Chapter 19). They can handle routine responses, heart easy comments, and flag the questions that need your personal touch. You stay present without being buried.

And accept that you will miss comments. You'll have days when you don't respond to anyone. That's fine. Consistent engagement over months and years matters infinitely more than perfect responsiveness on any given day. Do your best. Don't spiral about the gaps.

One more thing on sustainability: track your return commenters. Notice the names that show up repeatedly. When you see the same person on three, four, five videos in a row, that's not a coincidence. That person is investing in your channel. Acknowledge them. A simple "Good to see you back, [name]" costs five seconds and creates a connection that lasts months. I have regulars on both my channels who've been commenting for years. I know their names, their situations, their goals. That's not because I have superhuman memory, it's because I paid attention early, and it compounded.

AI INTEGRATION

Your Community Strategy Generator

Use this prompt to build a complete community engagement strategy for your channel:

PROMPT: YouTube Community Builder

Help me develop a community-building strategy for my YouTube channel.

- My channel niche: [YOUR TOPIC/INDUSTRY]

- My target audience: [WHO YOU SERVE]

- Current subscriber count: [NUMBER]

- Average comments per video: [NUMBER]

- What my audience is trying to achieve: [THEIR GOAL]

- My channel's core values: [WHAT YOU STAND FOR]

Please provide:

1. A suggested identity/name for my community members

2. Five end-of-video questions to spark comments (specific to my niche)

3. Ten community post ideas (mix of polls, questions, behind-the-scenes)

4. Response templates for common comment types (questions, praise, criticism)

5. Three ways to feature community members in my content

6. A weekly community engagement schedule (what to do each day)

Focus on genuine connection, not vanity metrics.

This gives you a full playbook you can implement this week. Revisit it every quarter to refresh your approach. AI is great at generating ideas you wouldn't have thought of on your own, but you still have to show up and actually engage. The prompt writes the plan, you execute it.

CASE STUDY

Elena: From Talking Into a Void to Leading a Movement

Elena was a financial planner with a YouTube channel stuck at about 4,500 subscribers. Her content was solid. Production quality was fine. She posted consistently. But engagement was basically nonexistent. Videos would get a handful of comments, mostly generic "Great video!" or transactional questions with no conversation behind them.

"I felt like I was talking into a void. I'd put hours into creating content and get almost nothing back. No conversations. No connection. Just views that disappeared."

Elena's problem was simple: she was broadcasting, not building. She'd post a video and move on. Never responded to comments. Never asked questions. Never used the Community tab. Her channel was a one-way loudspeaker.

We implemented five changes.

1. **Respond to every comment within 24 hours of publishing.** Not "Thanks!" but actual responses, answering questions, asking follow-ups, engaging with what people said.

2. **End every video with a specific question.** "What's the one money habit you're trying to build this year? Tell me in the comments. I read every single one."

3. **Post to the Community tab three times a week.** Polls about financial topics, behind-the-scenes of her recording setup, quick tips too short for full videos.

4. **Turn great viewer questions into videos, mentioning the commenter by name.** She started a monthly "Wins Wednesday" post where viewers shared financial wins, and she celebrated them publicly.

5. **Give her community an identity:** "The Financial Freedom Crew." She referenced them as a group: "As the Financial Freedom Crew knows, building wealth isn't about restriction, it's about intention."

Six months later:

- Comments per video went from 8–12 to 45–70

- Subscribers jumped from 4,500 to 11,200

- Community post engagement hit 200–400 interactions per post

- She identified 180+ repeat commenters who showed up on three or more videos

- Client inquiries tripled with no increase in content volume

The biggest result? Her community members started sharing her videos in Facebook groups, recommending her in Reddit threads, tagging friends. She never asked them, they did it because they felt ownership in what she'd built.

"The time investment is real, maybe 30–40 minutes a day on engagement. But the return is exponential. I used to feel like a content machine. Now I feel like I'm leading a movement. These aren't just viewers, they're people I know by name who are on a journey together."

CRAZY SIMPLE ACTION

Launch Your Community Strategy

Complete this exercise to transform your channel from a broadcast platform into a gathering place. All five parts. One sitting. No excuses.

Part 1: Define Your Community Identity (10 minutes)

- What are my community members trying to achieve? _______________

- What values do we share? _______________

- What could I call my community? _______________

- What makes someone "one of us"? _______________

Part 2: Set Your Engagement Commitment (5 minutes)

- My comment response window: _______________ (e.g., within 24 hours of publishing)

- Morning engagement slot: _______________ (time + duration)

- Evening engagement slot: _______________ (time + duration)

- Total daily engagement time: _______________ minutes

Part 3: Create Your Question Bank (15 minutes)

Write five end-of-video questions specific to your niche:

1. _______________

2. _______________

3. _______________

4. _______________

5. _______________

Part 4: Plan Two Weeks of Community Posts (15 minutes)

- Week 1 Monday:

  ____

- Week 1 Wednesday:

  ____

- Week 1 Friday:

  ____

- Week 2 Monday:

  ____

- Week 2 Wednesday:

  ____

- Week 2 Friday:

  ____

Part 5: Baseline Your Metrics (5 minutes)

- Current average comments per video: _________________

- Repeat commenters I recognize by name: _________________

- 30-day goal for comments per video: _________________

- 90-day goal for community post engagement:

____

Community building compounds like content does. The first few weeks feel like nothing is happening. You respond to a handful of comments. Your Community tab posts get 12 interactions. Your questions get three responses. Keep going. Those handfuls of engaged viewers become dozens, then hundreds. They become your referral network, your social proof, and the reason your channel keeps growing, even on the weeks you don't feel like showing up.

In Chapter 22, we'll explore repurposing your YouTube content across other platforms, maximizing reach without multiplying your workload.

CHAPTER 22
Repurposing Content: Maximum Reach, Minimum Effort

OPENING HOOK

A coaching client of mine, a real estate agent in Austin, sent me a screenshot last year that made me want to throw my laptop. She'd spent an entire Saturday filming a property tour. Good lighting. Solid script. Clean edit. She published it on YouTube, got 1,200 views over the first week, and moved on to the next video.

That same week, another agent in her market filmed a nearly identical tour, same neighborhood, similar price point. But this agent's team extracted three 45-second vertical clips from the long-form video, posted them on Instagram Reels and TikTok, turned the script into a LinkedIn carousel, emailed the video to her list with a personal note, and embedded it on a blog post optimized for Google. Total extra time? About 90 minutes, most handled by her VA.

That second agent got 1,100 views on YouTube, about the same. But she also pulled 8,400 views across Reels, 3,200 on TikTok, 67 LinkedIn engagements, 340 email opens, and ongoing organic traffic to her website for months. One video shoot. Five platforms. Twelve total pieces of content.

The first agent did four hours of work and got 1,200 impressions. The second did about five and a half hours and got over 13,000. Same content. Same quality. Completely different return on investment.

I spent years making the first agent's mistake. I'd pour effort into a YouTube video, publish it, and move on like the job was done. It wasn't until I watched smaller creators with weaker content consistently outgrow me on other platforms that I realized what I was leaving on the table. Every video you publish without repurposing is a half-finished job. You did the hard part already, the filming, the editing, the expertise. Repurposing is just finishing what you started.

THE FRAMEWORK

YouTube Is the Hub. Everything Else Is Distribution.

Here's how to think about this. YouTube is where you create. It's the engine. Long-form videos build deep authority, rank in search for years, and generate the trust that actually converts strangers into clients. That doesn't change. YouTube stays your primary platform and your main time investment.

Other platforms are distribution channels. They exist to take the work you already did on YouTube and put it in front of people who would never have found you otherwise. LinkedIn reaches your professional network. Instagram and TikTok reach younger demographics and casual scrollers. Email reaches your warmest audience directly. A blog captures Google search traffic. A podcast reaches people who consume content while driving or exercising.

The mistake most creators make is treating every platform like it needs original content. That's a recipe for burnout. You don't need seven content strategies. You need one content strategy with a distribution plan. YouTube is the strategy. Everything else is distribution.

Pick two platforms beyond YouTube. That's it. Two. I don't care how many gurus tell you to be everywhere. You will burn out trying to maintain five platforms with original content on each. Two spokes that you do consistently will outperform six spokes you do sporadically every time.

How do you pick your two? Go where your audience already is. If you serve business professionals, LinkedIn is obvious. If you serve consumers, Instagram probably makes sense. If you want to reach people passively, email and a blog are hard to beat. If your audience skews younger, TikTok deserves attention. Don't guess, think about where your best clients or customers actually spend their time online.

How to Adapt Content for Each Platform

Cross-posting the same thing everywhere is lazy, and it shows. Each platform has its own culture, format, and expectations. The good news? Adapting content is way faster than creating it from scratch.

LinkedIn. This is your professional credibility play. Take the main insight from your video and write a 150–250 word text post. Start with a hook that stops someone mid-scroll. Share the insight, add context or a personal take, and end with a question that invites conversation. Don't just paste your video link. LinkedIn buries external links. Write the post, get the engagement, and mention the video in the comments if people want to go deeper.

Instagram. Vertical short clips are the move. Have your editor export two or three 30–60 second vertical clips of your best moments, these become Reels. Add captions because most people watch without sound. You can also turn key points into carousel graphics using Canva. Quote cards from your best one-liners work well in Stories.

TikTok. Very similar to Instagram Reels, but TikTok rewards a slightly more raw, direct-to-camera feel. YouTube Shorts can often cross-post to TikTok with minor tweaks. If something performs well on YouTube Shorts, test it on TikTok too. Audiences overlap less than you might think.

Email. This is your most underrated distribution channel. Your email list is an audience you own, no algorithm decides whether they see your content. Send a short email when you publish: what the video covers, why it matters, and a link. Once a month, send a roundup of your best content. Keep it simple. People overcomplicate email.

Blog. Embed your YouTube video in a blog post with a written summary underneath. This captures Google search traffic YouTube alone might miss and keeps people on your website, where your lead magnets and contact forms live. Your video transcript, cleaned up and expanded, becomes the blog post. Two birds.

Podcast. Strip the audio from your YouTube video, add a 30-second intro explaining the format, and publish it as a podcast episode. People who would never watch a 15-minute video will listen while driving, exercising, or cooking. Same expertise, different consumption behavior.

The Workflow That Makes This Sustainable

Repurposing falls apart when it's not systematized. If you make decisions about what to repurpose and where every single week, you'll quit within a month. You need a process.

Step 1: Film with repurposing in mind. While filming your YouTube video, mentally flag two or three moments that could stand alone as short clips, a surprising statistic, a strong opinion, a quick tip. Zero extra time, but it saves your editor from hunting later.

Step 2: Extract clips and transcribe during editing. Your editor or VA exports short vertical clips during the YouTube editing process. They also run the video through a transcription tool like Descript or Otter.ai. Adds maybe 15–20 minutes to the workflow.

Step 3: Batch your repurposing. Set one block of time each week, maybe two hours, to process all repurposed content from that week's video. Write LinkedIn posts. Format the email. Queue the Reels. Schedule everything using Buffer, Later, or another tool. Batching prevents context-switching, which is where most time gets wasted.

Step 4: Prioritize your best content. Don't repurpose everything. Your best video this month probably deserves full treatment: clips, LinkedIn, email, blog post. A standard video might get clips and email. A weaker video might only get cross-posted clips. Match effort to quality.

The point: YouTube remains your primary creative effort. Repurposing should never eat into filming or editing time. If it does, you've overcomplicated it. Scale back to fewer platforms and simpler formats until it feels easy.

Here's a benchmark from my channels: a solid repurposing workflow adds about 20% more total effort for roughly 300% more reach. That math should make you angry about every video you've published without repurposing. Don't dwell on the past, start with your next publish and build the habit forward.

What Not to Do

- **Don't copy and paste the same caption across every platform.** LinkedIn users and Instagram users have completely different expectations. A three-paragraph thought leadership post works on LinkedIn. On Instagram, that same text gets ignored. Adapt the format and tone.

- **Don't repurpose before your YouTube content is solid.** If you're still figuring out your filming, scripting, and editing workflow, adding repurposing will overwhelm you. Get your YouTube rhythm locked in first, Chapter 14's content calendar exists for this. Once YouTube feels routine, then layer in repurposing.

- **Don't forget the callback.** Every piece of repurposed content should give people a reason to visit your YouTube channel. Not a desperate "please subscribe" plea. A genuine next step works better: *"If this was useful, the full breakdown covers three more strategies. Link in bio."* You're building a system where each platform feeds the others.

- **Don't obsess over metrics on repurposed platforms like you do on YouTube.** Your LinkedIn posts don't need to go viral. Your Reels don't need millions of views. Repurposed content serves one purpose: staying visible to potential clients across the platforms they already spend time on. If a LinkedIn post gets 40 impressions but one of those 40 people is a business owner who remembers your name three months later when they need your service, that post did its job. Repurposing is about cumulative visibility, not individual home runs.

Here's something that took me too long to learn. On my @GotCoach channel, I resisted repurposing for over a year because I thought it would dilute the brand. I wanted people to come to YouTube, period. What actually happened was the opposite. When I finally started posting clips on Instagram and writing about my coaching frameworks on LinkedIn, my YouTube subscriber growth accelerated. People discovered me on one platform and followed the trail back to the channel. Each platform wasn't competing with YouTube, they were feeding it. The hub-and-spoke model works because attention compounds across platforms in ways that are hard to measure but impossible to ignore once you experience it.

AI INTEGRATION

Your Content Multiplication Machine

Use this prompt after every video publish to generate a week's worth of repurposed content in about 10 minutes:

PROMPT: YouTube Content Repurposer

Help me repurpose my latest YouTube video for other platforms.

- Video title: [YOUR VIDEO TITLE]

- Video topic summary: [2–3 SENTENCES ON WHAT THE VIDEO COVERS]

- Key points covered:

  1. [POINT 1]

  2. [POINT 2]

  3. [POINT 3]

- Best quote or insight from the video: [MEMORABLE LINE]

- My target platforms: [YOUR 2 CHOSEN PLATFORMS]

- My lead magnet or CTA: [WHAT YOU WANT PEOPLE TO DO NEXT]

Please create:

1. A LinkedIn post (150–250 words) with a scroll-stopping hook

2. An Instagram caption with 5 relevant hashtags

3. An email to my list announcing this video (casual, brief)

4. Timestamps for key points to clip as Shorts/Reels

5. A blog post outline expanding on the video's main theme

Match each piece to the platform's native style. No generic copy-paste feel.

Run this for every video. The AI gives you a strong first draft for each platform. Spend five minutes refining each piece to match your voice, and you've got a full week of content from one prompt. Pair this with OpusClip or Descript to auto-generate your short clips, and your entire repurposing workflow takes under an hour.

CASE STUDY

David: One Video Becomes a Content Ecosystem

David was a business attorney with about 6,000 YouTube subscribers and a consistent weekly schedule covering legal topics for entrepreneurs. His content was sharp. His delivery confident. He generated three to four leads per month from YouTube alone.

The problem was obvious once he saw it: his potential clients, startup founders and small business owners, spent as much time on LinkedIn and in podcast apps as they did on YouTube. David wasn't in either of those places. His expertise existed in exactly one location online.

"I knew I should be on other platforms. But I was already maxed out making YouTube videos. Creating original content for LinkedIn, a podcast, and email felt like it would require cloning myself."

We didn't ask David to create more content. We built a repurposing system around what he was already making. His editor extracted two to three vertical clips during the YouTube edit. The audio track was stripped and uploaded as a podcast episode with a quick intro. A VA turned the transcript into one LinkedIn article and three shorter LinkedIn posts per video. The short clips went to Instagram Reels. An email went to his list every publish day.

From each YouTube video, David's system produced 12–14 pieces of content. His additional personal time investment? About 30 minutes per week reviewing and approving his team's work. The team spent roughly two hours per video on the repurposing workflow.

Six months in, the numbers told the story: LinkedIn followers went from 800 to 4,200. Podcast downloads hit 1,500 per month from zero. Instagram grew from 200 to 2,800. His email list nearly quintupled from 400 to 1,900. YouTube subscribers climbed from 6,000 to 9,500, partly because repurposed content drove traffic back to the channel. Monthly leads jumped from three or four to 12–15.

But the biggest result? Resilience. David's leads used to come 100% from YouTube. After six months of repurposing, it was 45% YouTube, 30% LinkedIn, 15% podcast, and 10% other sources. When YouTube's algorithm had a slow week, his business didn't feel it.

"I'm not creating more content. I'm distributing the same content more intelligently. My ideas reach five times as many people with maybe 20% more effort. Every video I published before without repurposing was leaving money on the table."

CRAZY SIMPLE ACTION

Build Your Repurposing System

Complete all four parts in one sitting. You'll walk away with a working system, not just good intentions.

Part 1: Choose Your Two Platforms (5 minutes)

- Where does my target audience spend time besides YouTube? ___________________

- My primary repurposing platform: ___________________

- My secondary repurposing platform: ___________________

- Why these two (be specific): ___________________

Part 2: Define Your Content Types Per Platform (10 minutes)

- Platform 1 (___________________):
  - What I'll create from each video: ___________________
  - How often I'll post: ___________________
  - Tool I'll use to schedule: ___________________
- Platform 2 (___________________):
  - What I'll create from each video: ___________________
  - How often I'll post: ___________________
  - Tool I'll use to schedule: ___________________

Part 3: Map Your Workflow (10 minutes)

- Who extracts short clips: ___________________ (me / editor / VA)

- Transcription tool: _________________ (Descript / Otter / YouTube captions)

- Repurposing batch day and time: _________________

- Who writes platform-specific posts: _________________ (me / VA / AI + me editing)

- Who schedules content: _________________

Part 4: Repurpose Your Last Video Right Now (20 minutes)

- Video I'm repurposing: _________________

- Best moment for a short clip (timestamp): _________________

- Main insight for a LinkedIn/text post: _________________

- Email subject line to announce the video: _________________

- Write the LinkedIn post or email draft now. Not tomorrow. Not next week. Do it now while the framework is fresh. The first one takes the longest. By the third or fourth video, the process becomes muscle memory, and your team handles 90% without your involvement.

In Chapter 23, we'll explore the **compound effect of consistency** and why the channels that win aren't the most talented or best-funded, they're the ones that kept showing up.

CHAPTER 23
Measuring Your YouTube ROI: Tracking What Actually Matters

OPENING HOOK

A coaching client called me last year, frustrated. She had been publishing YouTube videos for nine months, consistent schedule, good content, growing subscriber count. Her question: *"Aaron, is this actually working? Because I honestly can't tell."*

I asked how many leads YouTube had generated in the last quarter. She didn't know. I asked how many clients she'd closed from YouTube leads. She didn't know that either. I asked what her cost per client acquisition was from YouTube compared to other channels. Blank stare through the Zoom screen.

She had 6,000 subscribers and was spending 12 to 15 hours a week on YouTube. At her billing rate, that was $4,000 a week in opportunity cost, and she had absolutely no idea whether it was paying off.

That's not a YouTube problem. That's a tracking problem.

I've coached creators who celebrate hitting 10,000 subscribers while their business stays completely flat. I've also coached creators who quietly build six-figure client pipelines with 3,000 subscribers. The difference is never subscriber count. It's whether they've built a system to track what YouTube actually contributes to their business.

Views don't pay the bills. Subscribers don't pay the bills. Knowing how many clients walked through your door because of YouTube, and what those clients were worth, is the only number that matters.

Once you install proper tracking, the fog lifts. You stop guessing and start making decisions with actual data. You find out which videos generate leads and which just generate views. You find out whether your time investment makes sense. And you find out exactly where your funnel breaks down so you can fix the right thing instead of randomly tweaking everything.

THE FRAMEWORK

Forget Vanity Metrics. Track These Five Numbers.

I need you to temporarily forget everything YouTube Analytics tells you: views, watch time, subscriber count, impressions. Those are leading indicators. They might predict business results, but they aren't business results. A channel with amazing YouTube metrics and zero leads is failing. A channel with modest metrics and consistent leads is winning.

Here are the five numbers that actually determine whether YouTube is working for your business:

1. **Leads generated.** How many people gave you their contact information because of YouTube? Lead magnet downloads, consultation requests, contact form submissions, DMs referencing your videos, direct outreach that mentions your channel. This is the conversion point where anonymous viewers become known prospects you can follow up with.

2. **Consultations booked.** Of those leads, how many took the next step and booked a call or meeting? This measures the quality of your leads and whether your nurture sequence is doing its job. If you're generating leads but nobody books, the problem isn't YouTube, it's what happens after someone opts in.

3. **Clients acquired.** How many consultations turned into paying clients? This is the number that hits your bank account, real revenue from real people who found you through YouTube.

4. **Revenue attributed.** What's the total dollar value of those YouTube-sourced clients? Include both initial purchases and lifetime value if clients stick around. A real estate agent closing a $400,000 transaction from a YouTube lead tells a very different ROI story than a coach selling a $500 course.

5. **Cost per acquisition.** What does it cost you in time and money to acquire each YouTube client? This tells you whether YouTube is efficient compared to paid ads, networking, cold outreach, or whatever else you're doing. If YouTube clients cost $200 each and paid ad clients cost $800, that's a clear signal about where to invest.

Building Your Tracking System

You don't need fancy software. You need four things working together:

1. **Tag your traffic sources.** Every link from YouTube to your website should include UTM parameters so you know where traffic came from. Instead of linking to yoursite.com/guide, link to yoursite.com/guide?utm_source=youtube&utm_medium=video &utm_campaign=videoname. When someone downloads your guide, you know they came from YouTube and which specific video sent them. Most link shorteners and CRM tools make this easy to set up.

2. **Track lead sources in your CRM.** Your email service, CRM, or intake form should record where each lead originated. If you're using something like GoHighLevel or HubSpot, UTM data gets captured automatically. If your setup is simpler, add a "How did you find us?" dropdown to your forms with YouTube as a specific option.

3. **Ask during every consultation.** The most reliable attribution method is also the simplest. When someone books a call, ask: *"How did you first come across my work?"* When they mention YouTube, ask which videos they watched. Record the answer. This qualitative data catches leads UTM tracking misses, like the person who watched your video, Googled your name a week later, and came through your website with no tracking attached.

4. **Maintain a client source log.** Keep a Google Sheet with five columns: client name, source (YouTube, referral, search, other), which videos they mentioned, date acquired, and revenue generated. Update it every time you close a new client. This takes 30 seconds per entry and becomes the foundation for everything else.

The ROI Math

Once your tracking is in place, the calculation is simple:

Add up the revenue from all YouTube-sourced clients over a quarter. That's your YouTube revenue. Then calculate your total YouTube cost: your time (hours multiplied by your hourly value), team costs (editor, VA, designer), tools and software, and any paid promotion.

Plug those into the formula:

Revenue minus Cost, divided by Cost, multiplied by 100 equals your ROI percentage.

Example: You generated $15,000 in revenue from YouTube clients last quarter. Your costs were $3,000, including your time. That's ($15,000 − $3,000) ÷ $3,000 × 100 = 400% ROI. Every dollar you put into YouTube returned four dollars. That's a signal to invest more, not less.

If the formula makes your eyes glaze over, here's the simpler version: Did YouTube bring in more money than it cost you? Yes or no. Start there. You can get fancy with the math later.

What Good Numbers Look Like

After working with dozens of business YouTube channels, here are the benchmarks I use:

- **View-to-lead conversion:** 0.5% to 2% for most business channels. If 1,000 people watch your videos and 5 to 20 become leads, you're in the normal range. Above 2% is excellent and usually means your call to action and lead magnet are dialed in.

- **Lead-to-consultation conversion:** 10% to 25%. About one in five to one in ten leads should book a call if your nurture sequence is working. Below 10%? The problem is usually your follow-up emails, not your YouTube content.

- **Consultation-to-client close rate:** 20% to 50% for YouTube-sourced leads. As we covered in Chapter 18, YouTube leads are warmer than cold leads because they've already spent hours watching you demonstrate expertise. They should convert at higher rates than any other channel.

If you're below these benchmarks at any stage, that tells you exactly where to focus. Low view-to-lead? Improve your call to action and lead magnet. Low lead-to-consultation? Fix your nurture sequence. Low close rate? Revisit your consultation process from Chapter 18. The beauty of tracking each stage is that you stop guessing what's broken and start fixing the actual problem.

Why YouTube ROI Looks Worse Than It Is (At First)

Three things make YouTube ROI tricky to measure early on:

1. **Lag effect.** Someone might watch your videos for months before becoming a lead. The videos you publish today might generate clients six months from now. Early ROI calculations almost always underestimate the true performance of your channel because the full payoff hasn't arrived yet.

2. **Video library compounds.** Videos published a year ago still generate views, leads, and clients today. Every video you add increases your baseline lead generation without additional work. A YouTube library is like a savings account that earns compound interest. The balance keeps growing even when you stop making deposits.

3. **YouTube builds authority.** Referrals close faster when prospects can watch 50 videos proving your expertise before the first meeting. Speaking opportunities come from event organizers who found your channel. Brand recognition opens doors you can't attribute to a single video. These indirect benefits are real and massive but nearly impossible to capture in a spreadsheet.

For all these reasons, evaluate your YouTube ROI over quarters, not weeks. Give the compound effect time to work. A channel that breaks even in months one through six might deliver 300% returns in months seven through twelve as the library builds and the lag catches up.

Making Decisions From Your Data

Your tracking data should drive strategy, not just sit in a spreadsheet looking pretty.

If your ROI is strongly positive, invest more: more content, more team support, possibly paid promotion on your best-performing videos. Double down on what's working.

If your ROI is marginally positive, optimize before scaling. Find the leak in your funnel and fix it before pouring more water in.

If your ROI is negative after six months of consistent effort, diagnose where the breakdown is happening. Not enough views? That's a content or SEO problem. Views but no leads? That's a call-to-action problem. Leads but no clients? That's a sales process problem. Each one has a different fix.

And if your ROI is deeply negative with no improvement trend after a year? Get an outside opinion before you quit. I've never seen a business channel with solid fundamentals fail if the creator sticks with it long enough. Usually, the problem is one fixable bottleneck, not a fundamentally broken strategy.

One pattern I see constantly: creators who track ROI for the first time realize that one or two specific videos generate the majority of their leads. On my @GotCoach channel, about 15% of my videos drive roughly 70% of my consultation requests. Once I saw that pattern, I stopped guessing about what content to make and started reverse-engineering what those top-performing videos had in common: same topic cluster, same type of title, same call-to-action placement. Your data will reveal the same kind of pattern, the question is whether you're tracking closely enough to see it.

Compare YouTube's cost per acquisition to your other channels. If you spend $800 on Facebook ads to acquire a client and $200 on YouTube, that comparison should reshape your entire marketing budget. Most business owners I coach are shocked to discover YouTube clients cost a fraction of paid advertising clients, with the added benefit that YouTube clients already trust you before the first conversation.

AI INTEGRATION

Your ROI Analysis Assistant

Run this prompt quarterly to analyze your YouTube business performance and get specific recommendations:

PROMPT: YouTube Business ROI Analyzer

Analyze my YouTube channel's business performance and identify improvements.

My business: [WHAT YOU DO/SELL]

Average client value: $[AMOUNT]

Time period: [LAST 3 MONTHS / 6 MONTHS]

YouTube metrics:

- Total views: [NUMBER]
- New subscribers: [NUMBER]
- Videos published: [NUMBER]

Business metrics:

- Leads from YouTube: [NUMBER]
- Consultations booked: [NUMBER]
- Clients acquired: [NUMBER]
- Revenue from YouTube clients: $[AMOUNT]

Investment:

- Hours per week on YouTube: [NUMBER]
- Monthly team/tool costs: $[AMOUNT]

Please provide:

1. My conversion rates at each funnel stage
2. How my rates compare to benchmarks (0.5–2% view-to-lead, 10–25% lead-to-consultation, 20–50% consultation-to-client)

   o My YouTube ROI calculation
   o The biggest weakness in my funnel

o   Three specific actions to improve results

o   Projected results if I improve the weakest stage by 50%

Ten minutes to gather your numbers. Clear direction on where to focus. Run it every quarter and compare results over time. That trend line matters more than any single quarter's number.

CASE STUDY

Marcus: From "I Think It's Helping" to $152,000 in a Quarter

Marcus was a business consultant who had been creating YouTube content for fourteen months. He had about 7,800 subscribers and averaged 2,000 to 3,000 views per video. His sense was that YouTube was "probably working" for his business, but he couldn't prove it.

"People mention my videos all the time in conversations. But if you asked me to put a dollar figure on what YouTube was actually generating, I'd have no idea. I was operating on vibes, not data."

Marcus was spending 12 to 15 hours a week on YouTube. At his consulting rate of $250 an hour, that represented $3,000 to $4,000 a week in opportunity cost. Without knowing his actual ROI, he couldn't make an informed decision about whether to scale up, scale down, or change strategy entirely.

We installed four things: UTM-tagged links in every video description so he could track which videos sent traffic; a required "How did you find me?" field on his intake form; a standard opening question for every discovery call: *"How did you first come across my work?"*; and a simple Google Sheet logging every new client with their source and revenue value.

After 90 days of tracking, the picture snapped into focus. Out of 78,000 views, he generated 127 leads, booked 34 consultations, closed 11 clients, and produced $88,000 in revenue. His total YouTube investment, including time, was about $41,200, a 114% ROI. More than doubling his money.

But the real insight was in the funnel breakdown. His lead-to-consultation rate was 27%, healthy. His close rate was 32%, solid. But his view-to-lead conversion was 0.16%, well below the 0.5% benchmark. The bottleneck was obvious: plenty of people watched his videos, but almost none took the next step to become leads.

We focused everything on that one stage: stronger calls-to-action, a more compelling lead magnet, better placement in descriptions, and verbal mentions of the lead magnet mid-video instead of just at the end.

The following quarter: 82,000 views, about the same, but leads jumped from 127 to 287, clients went from 11 to 19, and revenue hit $152,000.

"I spent fourteen months guessing. Three months of tracking told me exactly what to fix. That one change basically doubled my revenue. I will never operate blind again."

CRAZY SIMPLE ACTION

Build Your Tracking System Today

All four parts. One sitting. You'll walk away with a working system, not a to-do list.

Part 1: Set Up Source Tracking (20 minutes)

Create a UTM-tagged link for your lead magnet:

yoursite.com/[page]?utm_source=youtube&utm_medium=video& utm_campaign=[name]

Your tagged link:

____

Add a 'How did you find me?' field to your intake form: ☐ Done

Write your consultation opening question:

____

Part 2: Create Your Client Source Log (10 minutes)

Open a new Google Sheet. Create five columns: Client Name, Source (YouTube / Referral / Search / Other), Videos Mentioned, Date Acquired, Revenue Generated. Bookmark it. This is your YouTube ROI dashboard from now on.

Spreadsheet created and bookmarked: ☐ Done

Part 3: Baseline Your Numbers (15 minutes)

Estimate these for the last 90 days. Best guesses are fine for your first baseline.

- Total YouTube views: _______________

- Leads from YouTube (estimate): _______________

- Consultations from YouTube leads: _______________

- Clients from YouTube: _______________

- Revenue from YouTube clients: $_______________

Part 4: Calculate Your Starting ROI (10 minutes)

- Hours per week on YouTube: _______________ x 12 weeks = _______________ total hours

- Your hourly value: $_______________

- Time cost: $_______________

- Team/tool costs (90 days): $_______________

- Total investment: $_______________

  ROI = (Revenue − Investment) ÷ Investment × 100 = _______________%

  Quarterly review date (put it in your calendar now): _______________

From today forward, you stop guessing. You track every lead source. You log every YouTube client. You calculate your ROI quarterly. Most creators never do this, they operate on feelings instead of data. That ends today. When you can see exactly what YouTube contributes to your business, every decision you make about content, time investment, and strategy becomes sharper.

In Chapter 24, we'll bring everything together with your 90-day roadmap: the step-by-step plan for launching your channel and building toward your first 10,000 subscribers.

CHAPTER 24
Your 90-Day Roadmap: From Here to 10,000 Subscribers

OPENING HOOK

Scott Himelstein had been "on YouTube" for twelve years. Twelve years. In that time, he'd accumulated 200 subscribers. His videos were inconsistent, sometimes market updates, sometimes listing tours, sometimes random thoughts about the industry. No strategy. No system. No measurable results.

When he told me that number during our first coaching call, I almost didn't believe it. Twelve years is a long time to do something with nothing to show for it. But his situation was more common than you'd think. Plenty of creators have YouTube channels. Almost none of them have YouTube systems.

Scott committed to 90 days. Not 90 days of hoping things would get better. Ninety days of following a specific plan with specific actions in a specific sequence. No shortcuts. No skipping steps. No "I'll get to that next week" on the foundation work.

In those 90 days, Scott went from 200 subscribers to 2,000. He published 14 videos. His lead magnet got 156 downloads. He booked 23 consultations and closed four clients for $87,000 in commissions, all from a channel he'd let sit dormant for over a decade.

The difference wasn't talent. Scott's on-camera skills didn't magically improve in three months. The difference was structure. He had a plan that told him exactly what to do each week, so he stopped guessing and started executing. That's what this chapter gives you: not motivation, not inspiration, a plan. Week by week, phase by phase, from wherever you are right now to a functioning YouTube channel that generates real business.

THE FRAMEWORK

Phase 1: Foundation (Weeks 1–2)

Don't publish anything yet. I'm serious. The biggest mistake I see is creators rushing to upload their first video before their foundation is set. You end up with a channel that looks half-built, a lead magnet that doesn't exist, and content aimed at nobody in particular. Two weeks of preparation saves you months of backtracking.

- **Days 1–2: Lock down your business model.** Define how YouTube generates revenue for your business. Go back to Chapter 4 if you need a refresher. Are you driving client acquisition? Product sales? Consulting inquiries? Get specific. "Grow my business" is not a business model. "Generate 10 buyer leads per month through neighborhood tour videos" is.

- **Days 3–4: Set up your channel.** Complete the seven elements from Chapter 6: channel name, profile picture, banner, description, links, default upload settings, and a placeholder for your channel trailer. Your channel should look like a professional operation before anyone sees it. First impressions matter, a channel with a blank banner and no description screams "I just started this yesterday."

- **Days 5–7: Build your lead magnet and capture system.** This is not optional. Review Chapter 17 and build your lead magnet before you publish a single video. A checklist, guide, or template, something genuinely useful that people trade their email for. Set up your capture page and connect it to your email service. Publishing videos without a lead magnet in place means generating attention with nowhere to send it.

- **Days 8–12: Research topics and plan your first month.** Use the five methods from Chapter 7 to find 12 topics your audience is actively searching for. Twelve gives you three months of weekly content. Develop working titles for your first four videos using Chapter 8 principles. Sketch thumbnail concepts. Don't aim for perfection, aim for good enough to start.

- **Days 13–14: Prepare your equipment and space.** Set up your filming area. Test your camera, lighting, and audio. Record a practice video and watch it back. Make adjustments. Get comfortable with the mechanics so that when it's time to film for real, you're not simultaneously learning your equipment and trying to deliver content.

Phase 2: Launch (Weeks 3–6)

Now you publish. The goal here is not perfection, it's establishing a rhythm and learning from real data. Your first videos will be your worst videos. That's not failure. That's exactly how this works.

- **Week 3:** Film, edit, and publish your first video. Use the hook formulas from Chapter 9 and the structure frameworks from Chapter 10. Film two videos in the same session if you can, batch filming saves enormous time because you only set up and break down once. Edit using the workflow from Chapter 12. Create thumbnails. Write descriptions using the template from Chapter 13.

When your first video goes live, pin a comment with your lead magnet link. Share it on your other social channels. Respond to every single comment within 24 hours. The engagement pattern you establish now sets the tone for your entire channel.

- **Weeks 4–6:** Establish your rhythm. Publish one video per week on the same day at the same time. I don't care which day, pick one and stick to it. Wednesday at 9 AM. Saturday at noon. Consistency trains your audience to expect you and trains the algorithm to promote you.

By the end of week six, you should have four published videos, a consistent publishing day, your first lead magnet downloads (even if just a handful), initial analytics data to learn from, and a feel for your content creation rhythm. If you have all five of these, you're ahead of 90% of creators at this stage.

Phase 3: Optimize (Weeks 7–10)

Four videos give you enough data to start making informed decisions instead of guessing. This is where most creators plateau, they keep doing the same thing without examining what's working.

- **Week 7:** Conduct your first real analytics review. Sit down with YouTube Analytics and answer four questions: Which video has the highest click-through rate, and what made that thumbnail and title work? Which video has the highest average view duration, and what made that content engaging? Where exactly do viewers drop off in your retention graphs? And how many leads has your lead magnet generated so far?

These answers should directly shape your next batch of content. If your neighborhood tour got three times the views of your market update, that's data telling you something, listen to it.

- **Weeks 8–10:** Iterate based on what you learned. Keep publishing weekly while implementing improvements. Strengthen your hooks where retention drops. Test different thumbnail styles on underperforming videos. Improve your call to action based on lead conversion rates. Start posting to the Community tab two or three times a week to build engagement between uploads.

By week ten, you should have eight published videos, a clear understanding of which content resonates, improved thumbnails and hooks based on actual data, a growing email list, and the first signs of a real community forming in your comments.

Phase 4: Accelerate (Weeks 11–13)

The final phase is about building momentum and setting up the systems that carry you beyond 90 days.

- **Week 11:** Increase output. If weekly publishing feels sustainable, test bumping to twice a week. If weekly still feels like a stretch, stay there but improve batching efficiency from Chapter 14. Also, create your first YouTube Short from your best-performing video. One Short. See how it performs before committing to a regular Shorts schedule.

- **Week 12:** Lock down the business side. Install your ROI tracking system from Chapter 23. Set up UTM-tagged links. Add source tracking to your intake forms. Review and improve your email nurture sequence. If you haven't booked a consultation from YouTube yet, examine where your funnel breaks down. Is it views to leads? Leads to consultations? Fix the specific bottleneck.

- **Week 13:** Plan your next 90 days. Take an honest look at your first 90 days. What content performed best? What didn't work? Research your next 12 topics. Set specific goals for the next quarter: subscriber targets, lead targets, client targets. The plan for days 91 through 180 should be informed by everything you learned in days 1 through 90.

What Realistic Progress Looks Like

Let me set honest expectations so you don't quit over a misunderstanding about timelines.

After 90 days of consistent effort, most business channels see 200 to 1,000 new subscribers. Some niches move faster, some slower. Business content builds smaller but more valuable audiences than entertainment content. Don't compare yourself to a guy doing prank videos.

Total views across your videos will typically land between 5,000 and 20,000. Early videos get fewer views. Later videos usually get more as the channel gains traction. The compound effect is real, but it takes time to show up.

Lead magnet downloads usually range from 20 to 100 in the first 90 days. Client acquisitions range from zero to five. Some creators land their first YouTube client in week eight; others take six months. The sales cycle in your industry matters more than your subscriber count.

These numbers are modest. They're supposed to be. YouTube is a long game. Scott didn't build a six-figure YouTube pipeline in 90 days, he built the foundation for one. Six months after our initial 90 days, he'd crossed 15,000 subscribers and was generating 15 to 20 buyer leads per month. The channel he'd neglected for twelve years became his primary source of business: more reliable than Zillow, more cost-effective than paid advertising, more valuable than cold calling.

The 90-day roadmap is a launchpad. What you build on it in months four through twelve is where the real results live.

One thing I want to be direct about: you will have a week somewhere in this 90 days where you want to quit. Maybe your third video gets 47 views. Maybe a comment stings. Maybe you watch your own footage and cringe. Every single creator I've coached has had that moment. The ones who made it through didn't have more motivation or thicker skin, they just had a plan that told them what to do next, so they did the next thing instead of spiraling. That's what this roadmap is for, not to inspire you, but to keep you moving when inspiration runs out.

AI INTEGRATION

Your Personalized 90-Day Planner

Use this prompt to adapt the roadmap to your specific situation, schedule, and constraints:

PROMPT: Personalized YouTube 90-Day Roadmap

Help me create a customized 90-day plan to launch my YouTube channel.

- **My business:** [WHAT YOU DO/SELL]

- **My target audience:** [WHO YOU SERVE]

- **My YouTube goal:** [LEADS / AUTHORITY / CLIENTS / ETC.]

- **Hours available per week for YouTube:** [NUMBER]

- **Current YouTube status:** [NEW / HAVE SOME VIDEOS / ETC.]

- **My biggest concern about starting:** [WHAT WORRIES YOU MOST]

Please create:

1. A customized week-by-week plan for 13 weeks

2. Specific milestones to hit at weeks 4, 8, and 13

3. The top 3 things I should prioritize given my time constraints

4. What I should NOT worry about in the first 90 days

5. How to handle my biggest concern

6. Realistic expectations for results in my specific niche

   Make the plan realistic for my available time.

If you only have five hours a week, your plan looks different than someone with twenty. The AI helps you prioritize ruthlessly instead of trying to implement everything at once. Run this before you start Week 1, and revisit it anytime you feel overwhelmed about what to focus on next.

CASE STUDY

Scott: From 12 Years of Nothing to a Six-Figure YouTube Pipeline

I opened this chapter with Scott's 90-day numbers, but the full story is worth telling because it captures everything this book is about.

"I knew YouTube could work. I'd watched other agents in my market build entire businesses from it. But I couldn't figure out what I was doing wrong. I felt like I was shouting into the void for twelve years."

What Scott was doing wrong was everything and nothing. His individual videos weren't terrible. His on-camera presence was fine. His knowledge was solid. But he had no system. He'd post when he felt inspired, which meant three weeks could go by between videos. He never touched his descriptions or tags. He never had a lead magnet. He never looked at analytics. He was treating YouTube like a hobby while hoping it would perform like a business tool.

- **Weeks 1–2:** Scott rebuilt his foundation from scratch. He clarified that YouTube would generate buyer leads for his real estate practice. He optimized every element of his channel, built a "First-Time Buyer's Checklist" as his lead magnet, set up the capture page connected to his CRM, and researched twelve topics his local audience was actively searching for.

- **Weeks 3–6:** He published his first four videos, one per week, every Wednesday at 9 AM. These weren't his best work, but they were strategic: keyword-targeted topics with proper hooks, structured using the 7-part framework, and every video promoted his lead magnet. He responded to every comment within 24 hours, even the simple "nice video" ones.

- **Weeks 7–10:** Analytics revealed that his neighborhood tour videos had the highest retention by a wide margin. He doubled down, tested new thumbnails on early videos, and improved hooks based on exactly where the retention graphs showed drop-off. Lead magnet downloads grew from 3 per week to 12.

- **Weeks 11–13:** Scott increased to twice-weekly publishing. He created his first YouTube Short from a neighborhood tour video, which pulled 15,000 views, more than all his long-form videos combined at that point. He installed proper ROI tracking and closed his first YouTube-sourced client: a couple who'd watched seven of his videos over three weeks before reaching out.

Ninety days: 200 → 2,000 subscribers, 14 videos published, 156 lead magnet downloads, 23 consultations, 4 clients, $87,000 in commissions.

But the number that mattered most was what came after. Six months in, Scott had 15,000 subscribers and was generating 15–20 buyer leads per month exclusively from YouTube. By the end of his first full year, YouTube had generated over $300,000 in revenue. The channel he'd ignored for twelve years became the most reliable, cost-effective lead generation tool he'd ever used.

"The roadmap gave me structure. Before, I was posting randomly and hoping something would happen. Once I had a system, a specific plan for each week, everything changed. I stopped overthinking and started executing. That clarity was the whole difference."

CRAZY SIMPLE ACTION

Your Commitment

This is the most important exercise in the book. Everything else was information. This is a decision. Fill it out, sign it, and put it somewhere you'll see it every day.

Part 1: Your Why

I'm building this YouTube channel because:

____

The business result I need from this:

____

Part 2: Your Schedule

Videos per week: _______________

Publishing day: _______________

Hours per week dedicated to YouTube: _______________

Content creation day/time: _______________

Part 3: This Week's Actions

Action 1 (due by _______________):

____

Action 2 (due by _______________):

____

Action 3 (due by _______________):

____

Part 4: Accountability

I will share this commitment with:

____

I will review my progress every: _______________

If I miss a week, I will:

____

Part 5: Sign It

I, _______________________________, commit to following this 90-day roadmap.

I understand that consistency beats perfection. I will publish even when my videos aren't perfect. I will trust the compound effect. I will stay the course.

Signed: _______________________________ Date: _______________

One Last Thing

The next 90 days pass whether you build your channel or not. That's true for everyone who reads this book. Some will execute. Most won't. The ones who execute aren't smarter or more talented, they just decided to start and refused to stop.

You have everything you need. Not most of it. All of it. The strategy, frameworks, tools, AI prompts, case studies, and step-by-step systems. The only variable left is you.

Go build something.

END OF BOOK ONE

Continue your journey in *Book Two:Crazy Simple YouTube: Scaling to 100,000 Subscribers and Beyond*

Acknowledgments

I'm going to keep this short because you didn't buy this book to read about my feelings. But some people made this thing possible, and they deserve to see their names in print.

To my wife: thank you for tolerating the early mornings, the late nights, the garage studio takeovers, and the endless conversations about click-through rates at dinner. You never once told me this was a dumb idea, even when it probably looked like one. That patience is the reason two YouTube channels exist, a coaching business runs, and this book got finished. I love you more than any algorithm could measure.

To Tom Ferry: you gave me a stage before I had any business being on one. You saw a coach who happened to know YouTube and said, "Teach my people." That trust changed the trajectory of everything. The agents I've worked with through your ecosystem are proof that your model works, and I'm grateful to be part of it.

To Pawan, my video editor: four years of building two channels together is no small thing. You were there when VanLife was a hobby and Got Coach was an experiment. The late-night uploads, the thumbnail revisions, the "can we re-cut this intro one more time" texts, you helped build something real.

To my virtual assistants and team members who keep the machine running while I coach, speak, write, and occasionally sleep: you handle the hundred small things that make the big things possible. This book exists partly because you freed up the hours for me to write it.

To Daniel Kotula in Prague, who trusted the process when nobody in his market was doing YouTube the way I was teaching it: your results became the story I tell on stages. You proved the framework works across oceans.

To Rachel Smith, Leah Courage, Natalia Echeverri, and Patrick O'Connor: you let me use your channels as case studies, your wins as teaching moments, and your struggles as proof that this journey isn't always pretty. Every reader who sees themselves in your stories has you to thank for being willing to share them.

To Marcus, David, and every client and coaching member whose transformation appears in these pages, whether by real name or adapted for privacy: you trusted a process, did the work, and let me document the results. That's courage, and it makes this book infinitely more useful than theory alone ever could.

And to every coaching client I've ever worked with, whether you're in this book or not: you took a bet on yourself when most people just talk about it. You sat through strategy calls, filmed videos when it felt awkward, published when you weren't ready, and kept showing up when the views were low and the comments were empty. Some of you turned a dead channel into a six-figure lead pipeline. Some of you are still grinding through your first fifty videos. I respect both equally because both require the same thing: deciding you're going to do this and then actually doing it. You didn't just hire a coach, you became proof that the system works. Every framework in this book was tested on your channels, refined by your feedback, and validated by your results. This book is mine, but the evidence belongs to you.

To the 170,000 subscribers across @VanLife and @GotCoach who watched, commented, shared, and showed up: you are the living proof that the strategies in this book work. Every view, every comment, every "I found you on YouTube" email is a data point that kept me writing.

To the agents on those Tom Ferry webinars and training sessions who asked the hard questions, pushed back on my frameworks, and then went out and implemented anyway: your feedback made this book sharper. Your results made it credible.

To the creators and strategists whose work sharpened my thinking over the years: you know who you are. The YouTube ecosystem is better because people share what works instead of hoarding it.

And to you, the person holding this book: you didn't have to pick this one. There are a thousand YouTube guides out there, most recycling the same generic advice. You chose the one written by a guy who actually runs channels, actually coaches creators, and actually tracks the numbers. I don't take that lightly.

Now stop reading the acknowledgments and go publish a video.

Aaron Cuha

Park City, Utah

2026

About the Author

Aaron Cuha is a Master Certified Business and Real Estate Coach with over 15,000 hours of coaching experience and a track record of saying things on stage that make people uncomfortable, in the best possible way.

He runs two YouTube channels that serve as his personal testing grounds: @VanLife (120,000+ subscribers) and @GotCoach (50,000+ subscribers). Between them, he's tested every strategy in this book on his own channels before ever recommending it to a client. That includes posting a YouTube Short every single day for 365 consecutive days on Got Coach just to see what would actually happen. Most YouTube "experts" give advice based on what they've read. Aaron gives advice based on what he's done.

Over the years, he's guided hundreds of professionals, including real estate agents, mortgage brokers, coaches, consultants, and service business owners, to build client acquisition systems powered by YouTube. His frameworks have helped agents go from 200 subscribers to 15,000+ while generating six figures in YouTube-attributed revenue. He's taken consultants from zero leads to 20+ qualified inquiries a month. And he's proven repeatedly that you don't need expensive equipment to win. Several of his clients have built channels north of 200,000 subscribers using nothing but their phones, no external mic, no professional editing, no excuses.

Aaron is also a licensed real estate broker in twelve states and a coach and speaker within the Tom Ferry ecosystem, where he brings enterprise-level business strategy to creators who've been told that "just be authentic" counts as a growth plan. He's the author of *Origins & Outcomes* and integrates AI workflows, NLP, and DISC behavioral assessments into his coaching, because understanding how people communicate is just as important as understanding how the algorithm works.

Beyond coaching, Aaron runs a YouTube management business, where his team handles everything except recording for clients who want done-for-you channel growth. Managing dozens of channels across multiple industries has given him a perspective most YouTube educators lack: he doesn't just know what works in theory. He knows what works when a real estate agent in Weston, Florida has three hours a week and zero patience for complexity.

His philosophy is simple: YouTube success for business professionals is not about entertainment. It's about demonstrating expertise, building trust at scale, and creating systems that turn viewers into clients. The strategies that work for gaming channels and lifestyle vloggers will actively hurt professionals trying to build authority. This book exists because that distinction matters, and almost everyone ignores it.

When he's not coaching, creating content, or writing books that tell you the truth instead of what you want to hear, Aaron lives in Park City, Utah, where the mountains are tall and the advice is short.

Connect with Aaron

YouTube: @GotCoach | @VanLife

Website: crazysimpleyoutube.com | gotcoach.com

Coaching & Services: crazysimpleyoutube.com/work-with-me

Community: crazysimpleyoutube.com/community

If this book changed how you think about YouTube, Aaron wants to hear about it. Share your wins, your first video, your subscriber milestone. Tag @GotCoach. The best part of writing this book is seeing what you do with it.

Resources and Tools

Everything Referenced in This Book (and a Few Extras)

This isn't a generic tool list scraped from someone else's blog post. These are the exact tools I use across two channels with 170,000+ combined subscribers, the tools my coaching clients use, and the tools referenced throughout every chapter of this book. I've organized them by function so you can find what you need fast.

Prices are accurate as of early 2026. They will change. The principles behind why you need each tool won't.

One rule before you start shopping: Audio quality matters more than video quality. A $50 microphone upgrade will do more for your channel than a $2,000 camera upgrade. Start there.

1. Equipment and Gear

Chapter 5 breaks down the full equipment philosophy. Here's the quick-reference version organized by budget tier.

Starter Tier ($0–$500)

Item	Recommended	Price	Notes
Camera	Your smartphone (iPhone 14+ or Samsung S23+)	Free (you own it)	Shoot in 4K at 30fps. Use back camera, not selfie cam.
Tripod	UBeesize 67" Phone Tripod	$25–35	Phone + camera compatible. Remote shutter included.
Lavalier Mic	Hollyland Lark M2	$50–80	Wireless, 1000ft range, 48kHz/24bit. Best budget wireless mic in 2026.
Lavalier Mic (Alt)	DJI Mic Mini	$70–90	10g per transmitter, 400m range, 48hr battery with case. Ultralight.
USB Mic	Maono PD300X	$50–70	USB + XLR dual output. Grow into it. Clear vocal profile.
Lighting	Neewer 18" Ring Light	$40–60	Adjustable color temp. Phone mount built in.
Lighting (Alt)	Elgato Key Light Mini	$80	Portable, app-controlled, excellent for desk setups.
Teleprompter	PromptSmart Pro (app)	Free–$20	Voice-activated scrolling. Works on any tablet.
Backdrop	Clean wall or bookshelf	Free	Depth > decoration. Stand 3–4 feet from your background.

Growth Tier ($500–$2,000)

Item	Recommended	Price	Notes
Camera	Sony ZV-E10 II	$900–$1,100	Best vlogging camera in 2026. 4K, no crop, great built-in mic, flip screen.
Camera (Alt)	Sony ZV-1 II	$700–$800	Compact, excellent autofocus, wide-angle lens built in.
Lens	Sony 16–50mm f/3.5–5.6	$300–$350	Kit lens for ZV-E10 II. Versatile for talking head + property tours.
Microphone	Rode Wireless Go II	$250–$300	Dual-channel wireless. 200m range. On-board recording backup.
Microphone (Alt)	Rode VideoMic Pro+	$250	On-camera shotgun. Great for mobile/ outdoor shooting.
USB Mic	Shure MV7+	$250–$270	USB + XLR hybrid. Touch panel. Auto-level technology.
Lighting	Elgato Key Light Air (x2)	$130 each	Desk-mount, app-controlled, 2800K–7000K range.
Teleprompter	Parrot Teleprompter V3	$130–$160	Mounts on camera lens. Professional delivery improvement.
SD Card	SanDisk Extreme Pro 128GB	$20–30	V30 speed rating minimum for 4K recording.

Pro Tier ($2,000–$5,000+)

Item	Recommended	Price	Notes
Camera	Sony a6700	$1,400–$1,500	APS-C flagship. AI autofocus, 4K 120fps, pro-grade codecs.
Camera (Alt)	Sony a7C II	$2,100–$2,200	Full-frame. Exceptional low-light. Future-proof investment.
Lens	Sigma 16mm f/1.4	$350–$400	Fast aperture for background blur. Talking-head hero lens.
Lens (Alt)	Tamron 17–70mm f/2.8	$750–$800	All-in-one zoom. Property tours + talking head in one lens.
Microphone	Shure SM7B	$350–$400	Industry standard broadcast mic. Requires audio interface.
Audio Interface	Focusrite Scarlett 2i2 (4th Gen)	$170–$190	Pairs with SM7B. Clean preamps. USB-C.
Lighting	Aputure Amaran 200d	$250–$300	Daylight-balanced LED. Professional 3-point lighting.
Gimbal	DJI RS 4	$400–$500	3-axis stabilization. Essential for property tours and walkthroughs.
Drone	DJI Mini 4 Pro	$760–$960	Under 249g (no license needed). 4K. Property exterior aerials.
Action Cam	DJI Osmo Pocket 3	$350–$520	Built-in gimbal. 16mm wide. Quick B-roll capture.

2. Video Editing Software

Pick one and learn it. Switching editors every month is a trap. The best editor is the one you'll actually use consistently.

Tool	Best For	Price	Key Features
CapCut Desktop	Beginners + Shorts creators	Free (Pro: $8/mo)	AI captions, templates, auto-reframe for Shorts. Incredibly fast for simple edits.
Descript	AI-powered editing	$24–$33/mo	Edit video by editing text. Filler word removal. AI voice cloning. Studio Sound noise removal. Automatic transcription.
DaVinci Resolve	Free professional editing	Free (Studio: $295 one-time)	Color grading powerhouse. Full editing suite. Fusion for effects. No subscription.
Adobe Premiere Pro	Industry standard	$23/mo (Creative Cloud)	Most plugins, integrations, templates. AI features via Firefly. Steep learning curve.
Final Cut Pro	Mac users	$300 one-time	Magnetic timeline. Optimized for Apple silicon. Fast rendering.
FireCut	Premiere Pro AI plugin	$15–$30/mo	AI auto-cuts, silence removal, chapter detection inside Premiere Pro.

My recommendation: CapCut to start, Descript once you want AI-powered workflows, DaVinci Resolve if you want free and powerful.

3. AI Tools for Content Creation

AI isn't optional in 2026. It's the difference between spending 15 hours per video and spending 5. Every chapter in this book includes specific AI prompts. Here's the full stack.

Scripting, Strategy, and Research

Tool	What It Does	Price	How I Use It
ChatGPT (GPT-4o)	Script generation, brainstorming, research	$20/mo (Plus)	Content ideation, script outlines, title variations, description drafts.
Claude (Anthropic)	Long-form writing, strategy, analysis	$20/mo (Pro)	Deep content strategy, book writing, complex prompt chains, document analysis.
Google Gemini	Research, summarization, multimodal	Free–$20/mo	Analyzing competitor videos, summarizing trends, image-based research.
Perplexity AI	AI-powered research engine	Free–$20/mo	Sourced research for scripts. Real-time data with citations.

Shorts and Clip Creation

Tool	What It Does	Price	How I Use It
OpusClip	AI clips from long-form video	$19–$49/mo	Upload long-form, get 10–15 viral-scored Shorts auto-generated with captions.
Vidyo.ai	AI short-form clips	$30–$50/mo	Alternative to OpusClip. Good for batch processing multiple videos.
Revid.ai	AI video from text/URLs	Free–$29/mo	Text-to-video Shorts. Auto Mode creates daily content from your specs.

Audio and Voice

Tool	What It Does	Price	How I Use It
ElevenLabs	AI voice cloning and voiceover	$5–$99/mo	Clone your voice for repurposed content. Voiceovers for B-roll sequences.
Descript Studio Sound	AI audio cleanup	Included with Descript	Removes background noise, echo, room tone. Makes any mic sound professional.
Adobe Podcast AI	AI audio enhancement	Free (web-based)	Enhance Speech feature cleans recordings after the fact. Dead simple.

Thumbnails and Visual Design

Tool	What It Does	Price	How I Use It
Canva Pro	Design platform with AI features	$13/mo	Thumbnail templates, Magic Eraser, background removal, brand kit.
Photoshop (AI)	Advanced thumbnail design	$23/mo (Creative Cloud)	Generative Fill for backgrounds. Professional compositing.
Pikzels	AI thumbnail scoring	$9–$29/mo	Scores thumbnail effectiveness before publishing. Predicts CTR.
Remove.bg	Background removal	Free–$10/mo	One-click background removal for thumbnail cutouts.
Midjourney	AI image generation	$10–$30/mo	Custom thumbnail backgrounds, conceptual images, B-roll visuals.

Automation and Workflows

Tool	What It Does	Price	How I Use It
N8N	Open-source workflow automation	Free (self-hosted)–$24/mo	AI avatar generation, automated posting, content pipelines. My primary automation engine.
Zapier	No-code automation	$20–$70/mo	Connect GoHighLevel, Skool, email, YouTube. Trigger-based workflows.
Make.com	Advanced automation	$9–$29/mo	Complex multi-step scenarios. Alternative to Zapier with more flexibility.

4. YouTube Growth and Optimization

These tools are built specifically for YouTube creators. They handle the SEO, analytics, and optimization that YouTube Studio alone can't give you.

Tool	What It Does	Price	Why You Need It
TubeBuddy	SEO, A/B testing, workflow optimization	Free–$8/mo	Keyword Explorer, tag suggestions, thumbnail A/B testing, best time to publish. The one tool every creator should install.
VidIQ	Analytics, keyword research, AI coaching	Free–$17/mo	Views Per Hour tracking, competitor analysis, Daily Ideas, AI Coach. Great complement to TubeBuddy.
ViewStats	Performance analytics (by MrBeast's team)	Free–$10/mo	2,500x more data points than competitors. Viral prediction. Real YouTube performance data.
YouTube Studio	Native analytics and management	Free	Your command center. Retention curves, traffic sources, revenue tracking. Check it weekly, not daily.
Social Blade	Public channel analytics	Free	Track competitor growth rates, compare channels, identify trends.
Poppy AI	Competitor analysis + script generation	$15–$40/mo	Analyze competitor videos, generate scripts in your voice, hook templates.

5. Lead Generation and Business

YouTube views don't pay bills. These tools turn views into leads and leads into clients. Chapters 17 and 18 cover the full system.

Tool	What It Does	Price	How It Fits
GoHighLevel (GHL)	All-in-one CRM, funnels, automation	$97–$297/mo	My primary CRM. Landing pages, email sequences, pipeline management, appointment booking. Replaces 5+ tools.
Skool	Community platform	$99/mo	Courses + community in one. Where my coaching members live. Gamification built in.
Calendly	Appointment scheduling	Free–$12/mo	Embed in YouTube descriptions and landing pages. Reduces scheduling friction to zero.
ConvertKit (Kit)	Email marketing	Free–$29/mo	If you're not on GHL yet. Visual automation builder. Creator-focused.
Leadpages	Landing page builder	$37–$74/mo	Standalone landing pages if you need something outside your main CRM.
Stripe	Payment processing	2.9% + $0.30/transaction	Connects to GHL and Skool. Handles all subscription and one-time payments.
Carrd	Simple one-page websites	Free–$19/year	Quick link-in-bio pages or single lead magnets. Dead simple setup.

6. Content Planning and Project Management

Tool	What It Does	Price	How I Use It
Notion	All-in-one workspace	Free–$10/mo	Content calendars, video databases, SOPs, team collaboration. My second brain.
Google Sheets	Spreadsheets	Free	Content tracking, keyword databases, analytics dashboards, editorial calendars.
Monday.com	Project management	$9–$19/mo per seat	Team workflow management. Great for multi-channel operations.
Trello	Visual task management	Free–$10/mo	Kanban boards for video pipeline: Idea → Script → Film → Edit → Publish.
Google Drive	Cloud storage and collaboration	Free–15GB / $3+/mo	Script sharing, asset storage, team access. Where everything lives.

7. Repurposing and Distribution

Chapter 22 covers the full repurposing system. These tools make it possible to turn one long-form video into 15+ pieces of content.

Tool	What It Does	Price	Output
OpusClip	AI short-form clips from long-form	$19–$49/mo	10–15 Shorts per long-form video with viral scoring and captions.
Descript	Transcript → blog posts, social clips	$24–$33/mo	Export text for blogs, newsletters. Create audiograms.
Riverside.fm	Record remote interviews + clips	$19–$29/mo	Separate audio/video tracks. AI Magic Clips for short-form.
Headliner	Audiograms and social video	Free–$15/mo	Turn podcast audio into animated social videos.
Buffer / Hootsuite	Social media scheduling	Free–$15/mo	Schedule repurposed content across Instagram, X, LinkedIn, Facebook.
Synthesia	AI avatar videos	$22–$67/mo	Turn scripts into talking-head videos without filming. Multiple languages.

8. Learning Resources

The YouTube algorithm changes. The tools update. The strategies evolve. These are the resources I trust to stay current.

Resource	Type	Price	Why I Recommend It
Crazy Simple YouTube Community (Skool)	Coaching community	$47/mo	My community. Live calls, frameworks, templates, peer accountability.
YouTube Creator Academy	Official YouTube training	Free	Straight from the source. Algorithm updates, best practices, policy changes.
Think Media (Sean Cannell)	YouTube education channel	Free (YouTube)	Equipment reviews, strategy breakdowns, creator interviews.
Film Booth	Storytelling and production	Free (YouTube)	Best channel for understanding video storytelling structure.
Creator Booth	Business of YouTube	Free (YouTube)	Revenue strategies, sponsorship negotiation, creator business models.

9. Book Companion Resources

Every chapter in this book has companion materials available online. These include the full AI prompt libraries, downloadable worksheets, video walkthroughs, and templates referenced throughout the book.

AI Prompt Library: crazysimpleyoutube.com/prompts

Every AI prompt from every chapter, organized by function. Copy, paste, customize.

Action Step Worksheets: crazysimpleyoutube.com/worksheets

Printable versions of every Crazy Simple Action section, plus bonus planning templates.

Video Tutorials: @GotCoach on YouTube

Video walkthroughs of key concepts from the book. See the strategies in action.

Community Access: crazysimpleyoutube.com/community

Join the Crazy Simple YouTube community on Skool. Get feedback on your channel, ask questions, connect with other creators who are building alongside you.

Equipment Guide (Updated): crazysimpleyoutube.com/gear

Gear evolves faster than books can be reprinted. This page always has my current recommendations with affiliate links.

Work With Me: crazysimpleyoutube.com/work-with-me

Coaching, done-with-you strategy, or done-for-you YouTube management. From $47/month community access to full channel management.

One more thing. Tools don't build channels. You do. The creator with a smartphone and a $50 mic who publishes twice a week will outperform the creator with $10,000 in gear who publishes twice a month. Every single time.

Start with what you have. Upgrade when it's the bottleneck, not when it's the excuse.

Keep it crazy simple.

What's Next

A Preview of Book Two: Scale to Authority

You made it. Twenty-four chapters. A complete framework for building a YouTube channel that generates real business results. If you followed the action steps, you now have a channel that's set up to convert, a content strategy targeting the right audience, a publishing system that keeps you consistent, and a lead generation machine that turns viewers into clients.

But here's the thing nobody tells you about hitting your first 10,000 subscribers: the game changes completely.

The strategies that got you from zero to 10,000 will not get you from 10,000 to 100,000. The hustle-and-grind approach that works when you're doing everything yourself becomes the ceiling that holds you back. The content formats that built your initial audience start plateauing. The one-person operation that felt scrappy and efficient starts feeling like a bottleneck that's strangling your growth.

I know because I've lived it, twice, on two separate channels. And I've coached dozens of creators through the exact same transition. The problems at 10,000 subscribers are fundamentally different from the problems at 500. And they require fundamentally different solutions.

That's what Book Two is about.

Scale to Authority: 10,000 to 100,000 and Beyond

Book Two picks up exactly where this book ends and guides you through five phases of scaling a YouTube channel into a full media operation.

Part I: Monetization Mastery. Book One introduced you to revenue streams beyond client work. Book Two goes deep. The full revenue stack beyond AdSense. YouTube Partner Program features most creators ignore entirely, like memberships, YouTube Courses, and Shopping integration. How to attract and negotiate brand partnerships with real rate cards and frameworks. And the course and digital product empire model, including how this very book series connects to courses, community, and management services. You'll learn how to build multiple income streams so your YouTube business isn't dependent on any single source.

Part II: Team and Systems. This is where most creators stall. Book One taught you when to make your first hire. Book Two teaches you how to build the machine. Your first YouTube hire and how to avoid the mistakes I made with mine. The complete SOP library that lets a VA run your channel while you focus on creating. How to scale production with AI, including N8N automation, AI avatars, and the workflows I actually use on my own channels. Building a full media team with the right roles, the right structure, and performance-based compensation that aligns incentives. And for those thinking bigger: the YouTube management model, where you run channels for clients at $2,500–$5,000 per month.

Part III: Multi-Channel Domination. When do you launch channel two? How do you turn one video into fifteen pieces of content without burning out your team? How does email integration with tools like GoHighLevel turn your YouTube audience into an asset you actually own? I'll break down the complete content ecosystem using @VanLife and @GotCoach as case studies, including the cross-platform amplification strategy that compounds growth across every platform simultaneously. This section builds the YouTube Flywheel, where every piece of content you create feeds every other platform automatically.

Part IV: Advanced Growth. The viral video formula, and no, it's not luck. Engineered virality, trend-jacking, and the "big swing" strategy that separates channels that plateau at 20,000 from channels that break through to 100,000. Collaboration at scale with a value-exchange framework that makes bigger creators want to work with you. Paid amplification through YouTube Ads and promoted videos, with real ROI calculations. And the plateau-breaking diagnostic framework for when your channel hits a wall at 10K, 50K, or 100K, because each ceiling has a different cause and a different fix.

Part V: The Media Empire. This is where it gets personal. Psychology and mental resilience at scale, because nobody talks about creator burnout, imposter syndrome, and the comparison trap until it's already eating you alive. Deep-dive case studies from channels that crossed 100,000 subscribers, including the full journey of @VanLife at 120K and @GotCoach at 50K. Future-proofing your channel against AI evolution and platform risk. And your complete 12-month media empire blueprint, the roadmap for building something that lasts well beyond any single algorithm update.

This Book Was the Foundation. Book Two Is the Architecture.

Everything in *Crazy Simple YouTube* was designed to get you from zero to a real, functioning YouTube channel that brings clients through your door. If you've done the work, you have that now. You have skills, systems, and proof of concept.

Scale to Authority assumes you've built that foundation. It doesn't re-teach the basics. It doesn't remind you how to write a title or film a video. It starts at 10,000 subscribers and treats you like a creator ready to build something serious. Bigger teams. Bigger revenue. Bigger impact. And the mindset to sustain it without burning out or losing yourself in the process.

Same format you're used to: set-in-stone structure in every chapter, opening hooks that grab you, frameworks you can deploy immediately, AI integration with actual prompts, real case studies with real names and numbers, and Crazy Simple Action steps that move you forward in one sitting.

Twenty-two chapters. Five parts. Zero fluff.

Get Notified When Book Two Drops

Book Two is currently in production. If you want to be first in line when it launches, along with early-access pricing and bonus materials that won't be available at full release, head to:

crazysimpleyoutube.com/book2

Drop your email. That's it. You'll get notified the moment pre-orders open, plus a free chapter preview before anyone else sees it.

In the meantime, go implement what you learned in this book. Film the videos. Publish consistently. Build the lead system. Track the ROI. The best way to prepare for Book Two is to outgrow Book One.

Keep it crazy simple.

Aaron Cuha